# Ackn

MW00951598

I would first and foremost like to thank the almighty God for giving me the passion to put my strengths as well as my weaknesses on paper; for giving me the gift to create a story. I also would like to give a big thanks to my momma Bernadette and my father William for having me if they haven't created me, I wouldn't have been able to do this. I want to thank you guys for giving me life; may you both sleep in peace, I love and truly miss you two.

I have to give thanks to my sister Passha aka Peaches. You said I would make it happen and I did, baby girl I did it. I know your smiling down on me saying let them keep talking baby sis. May you rest in peace.

Gosh I have to acknowledge my old lady, lol; my grandmother Dreamer. When I get rich, the world will be yours. I love you so much you had me from three days old and you still keep me going granny. I did this one for you.

To all my friends, my real ones, I love y'all! Word is life. It doesn't matter what life throws at yawl stay blessed up.

This here is for my three princes, I did it. Isayha baby boy I got you. You're my first-born son, threw our ups and downs I wouldn't trade you in for my life... my twin, hold your head up boy, it's not your last stop you're just on a world tour. You'll be home soon, mommy loves you.

To my baby boy Jaylen, I know you were here with me by my side when I was tired, you said "Mommy get up you got this, I love you so much you can do anything you want.", remember that, just never give up.

To my last bundle of joy Ramel, you are my promise child. You promised me with every beat your heart beat in my stomach you would be good lol and now your around here shutting it down, I love you so much while I wrote this you seemed to kick my computer on the floor come give me all kinds of kisses all for my attention. Baby boy you will always have mommy's attention. I love you MJ.

I have to give a big acknowledgement to my husband Mel, I said for at least two years straight I wanted to bring my dreams of becoming a published author to reality. Every day you would say "Why don't I see you writing? You always bullshitting!" Lol "You aren't doing nothing and you have the time write." I would always grab a pen and paper and I just never got to it. I had so much going on it seems like the devil was holding me back. It was like I had no good days coming but through our bad days we have some amazing ones. I want to say thank you for never giving up on me even when I gave you reason, I truly can't thank you enough for being so supportive through all my demise. I kept going with this, I want to write a book and you had enough you went and brought me a laptop for my birthday. So, I thank you for being a great husband and dad as well as step-dad.

You pushed me harder and harder; you gave me some tough love and you took the time out to make my cover for my book as a surprise to show me how much you wanted my dream to come into a reality and you also helped me with the title. I love you Mel, we all we got and you know the rest is history. I did it daddy and no you can't get none, lol!

Love always, Mrs. H through good times and bad times.

# Introduction

This book is a story about a group of females and males growing up in different sections of the hood of New York, where the street lights never go off. they seem to have met up in ways you couldn't even image. Chica is a Bronx chick who lived in each borough. She was a tough chick and money hungriest female you ever came across. She ends up becoming friends with Reyna in Albion Correctional Facility, where they both were locked up for five years. They literally had the prison on lock, they both had wardrobes so tight you would have thought they were in the town and their friendship traveled into the town they ended up linking with Reyna old friend Peaches, and the three began to teach the streets if you crossed them, they would do 'em dirty. Let's get ready to take this shit to the street that never sleep.

# Table Contents

# Chapter 1

Today I have come to this conclusion, I am in this dark space. I have been trying to fight towards the light for so long. Every time I felt like I was getting close and closer to the light 'boom', it seems as if someone has blindfolded me and my hands are behind my back. I am trying to break free but I can't get lose, I became suffocated I couldn't breathe and my throat became dry, I could feel myself reaching for the sink gasping to get a drink of water, but I couldn't reach it. My hands are tied "Shit!" I say to myself jumping up, head sweating looking around noticing it was a dream.

Now I'm a woke and as if any goals I had intentions of, have all disappeared, and I have no recollection of anything. Now it's time to get up. She shook her head, she had these dreams plenty of times but they was becoming more frequent. Getting herself together, she had so much to do today and having a flashback of her past life was not gonna get to her today she thought. She has always been this girl everyone loved due to her being a female and how she moved around the hood like a dude; she got more money than most niggas. She didn't fear any man nor a female. Yet, she was softer than mister softy ice cream when her heart is involved. She used to melt to men, shit the way the dick would feel and make her body shiver when it's inside it was enough to make any bitch summit to a nigga.

Let me introduce myself; my name is Chica I am 27 years old, light skin and I am built like a cherry pie. Let's just say I am slim trim with a cute fat little booty stands at 5 feet and 7 inches and weigh 145 pounds. I seem to get attention from both males and females. I actually like the attention of both genders on me. I could do them both dirty if I fucked a nigga who didn't eat pussy, I could easily make a bitch sweet on me and have a bitch face all in my shit eating my ass till my juices ran all over her face like the water running out of a wishing well, niggas bitches loved me literally, she said smiling to herself. I solidified my fucking spot in the streets so long ago they knew I wasn't one to be fucked with period; anybody could get it no one was off limits. I had no errors and they knew I would do 'em dirty if I was fucking crossed, hands down. Of course, a few motherfuckers tried their hand and of course I had to do 'em dirty. She started thinking about this bitch she had to put the hands of god on.

"Yo Chica" this trick ass bitch by the name of Zamir called out, I turned around and looked behind me.

The look I gave this bitch, you would have thought she would have changed her mind, ugh I couldn't stand this thirsty ass bitch but I said a quick inside prayer because I was in a shitty ass mood. I knew if she said one fucking slick comment today would be the day me and my homie friendship would end. "Why the fuck is you calling me for?" I asked her, "I fuck with you?" I was confused this dusty ass trick calling me like we cool, she paused for a second and I could tell she didn't know what to say. She began to stutter a little but her face told me I was about to light her ass like the Fourth of July.

"Hello." I said because she was just standing there looking stupid. "Was sup wit you shouting my name like that it's nothing we could have to talk about." I said. "Really, I'm surprised of your response cause the way you around here tricking for treats you would have thought it was Halloween." I had to laugh, she really tried it and since she was begging for an ass beating all these years, today she was going to get it. I didn't give this bitch the chance to say another fuckin word, I was on her and down she went. I tore her ass up like a dog who was looking for his last supper. Bam, bam I beat this bitch face non-stop. Not a soul stopped it because they have seen so many bad results from someone trying to break up one of my fights. In a quick flash they would be up next to feel my raft. As I beat this bitch ass, I yelled at her, "So bitch you just had to test me, right?" I was asking her. Bam "Huh bitch? Answer me." I yelled. 'Bam bam." I kept banging this bitch head to the ground. I held off of this bitch for way to long she was a cousin of a friend of mines I told this nigga he better put that bitch in her place.

Mario tried and of course she didn't listen. She screamed and screamed "Help! Get this crazy bitch off me." "Oh, now you calling for help huh bitch, nah hoe this is what you wanted right," I kept beating that bitch even though I knew I was way in over my head because this was my boy cousin and I was damn near killing her and there was blood every fucking where. However, I had avoided her for way to long. I was becoming to think she thought I was soft, just to think that's how I thought she felt made me madder. I started choking this bitch like I wanted to kill this bitch. I knew sooner or later the fuck boys was coming a nosey motherfucker would call. Her bum ass sister tried to get me off her but my goons were on her. It was a fucking brawl going on fights all in the middle of the streets, ass out tits showing and niggas was loving it. Shit I knew this was about to hit the net, everything hit the net and I didn't give ah fuck because I had plenty of fights on the net. It was just another reminder to let bitches know that I would do anybody dirty period.

As I fucking thought, the fuck boys pulled up and here I go about to be cuffed and hauled off and to sit in that got damn central dirty ass bookings. Once I saw Officer Brown get out, I knew she was locking me up. I swear I was contemplating on running but I didn't want to be another black killed or an officer targeting practice. So, I just sat down while this dumb bitch was screaming, "She tried to kill me. I want to press charges." I started laughing I could not believe this hoe; but hey everyone isn't so tough when the tables turn. I watched as they attended to this bitch, I smiled because I'd been wanted that ass, the officer approached me I began to get up because I knew what was coming.

"Hello" he said, I just stood there looking at him, was he really saying hello knowing damn well he was about to lock me up. "Hello" I said, "You can have a seat ma'am", so I sat down. "Would you mind telling me what happened, because the young lady over there seems to be wanting to press charges on you for assault." I just laughed, this was unbelievable I thought to myself 'she blood and yet she supposed to be a gangster'. "Look officer, do what you feel," and I didn't say another word. He said, "Look if you wish to cross complaint, both of you will be arrested." I looked him straight in his face, "Hell no," I'll take this one head on; however I'm going to do her dirty when I get out." Before he could respond here comes this thirsty ass Officer Brown. "Stand up, your black ass is going to jail." As I got put in the damn police car, I spit in Officer Brown's; face I hated that bitch.

She had a thing for locking me up, like this bitch wanted to eat my pussy or some shit. as I kneeled down to get in the cop car everybody had their phones out, I pulled my head back from going in the car and I yelled "Do 'em dirty bitches." Officer Brown shoved me in the car "Ahh ah, bitch!" I screamed. She started beating me with her knight stick. "Ahh!" I kept screaming "Bitch, I am going to kill you." she hit me again then closed the door while the other fucking fuck boys cleared the block out. I knew I was in for a beaten once I was pulled away. I just smiled cause this bitch is being put in a fuckin ambulance, "I'm satisfied." I said to myself, "Do 'em dirty bitch."

I knew from then on, I had to get out of B. K or I was going to catch another bid. After doing five years in an upstate correctional facility, I knew for sure that wasn't where I wanted to be again for another five years. Albion

Correctional Facility was not going to be my next stop period.

I moved from Brooklyn after living there for a couple years. I was there living with my sister when I had gotten released from prison. She was the only person who didn't turn her back on me. Although I haven't seen her since because things got heated but that's my sister and I love her. We just needed our space, so I had to leave.

# Chapter 2

## WHERE IT ALL BEGAN

I moved to the Bronx where I met this older dude when I say he was tall with this caramel complexion, a set of the most perfect white teeth I have ever seen and his smile seemed to make my panties seem invisible. I came just from the thought of his sexy ass lips sucking all over this fat pussy. Lordt I wanted to just say "Fuck me on a side street some damn where."

His name was Jamir and we chatted for a second. I gave him my number and then I kept it moving. I really wasn't into older men because they always had game and I wasn't for the bullshit, but his smile was everything. He was a smooth talker. Everything he said and the way it came out of his mouth made me want to try his dick cause that's all I really wanted.

"Was sup Chica you trying to pull-up to the concert with us," my home girl Peaches asked me while we smoked on my bed relaxing. "Hell, yea." I responded. "So whose going to be there?" I questioned. "Girl, Quan, JoJo and Nate and you know when they came in town to perform, they bring the city out." Peaches said laughing. "Hell yea, I'm always down you know me any where there's going to be money count Chica in!" I said and we slapped five. "Was sup with Candy and Reyna they Pullin up with us?" I asked Peaches because we always had the spot jumping. "Hell yea we rolling hard you know our motto." We both yelled "Do 'Em Dirty! you know we don't move unless we all move."

"Chica why do niggas all think we were some thot ass chicks?" Peaches asked. "I guess because we had another agenda for they ass and they know for a fact if they come, they have to come correct. Peaches fuck-niggas they just mad because they cannot afford us and that's cool fuck 'em." Chica said laughing. "Girl now past the blunt. We all got burnt by some niggas ever since you know we vowed to do 'em dirty plain in simple."

"I really hope this nigga Jay let you go Chica cause bitch we trying turn up and not turn up on your nigga," Peaches said in a real tone cause we were trying to enjoy ourselves, and I do not want nothing to ruined it .I just laughed cause my dude Jay didn't accept me hanging out with my girls cause he knew my girls was out to body everything because we all had banging bodies and a mean sex appeal. I played along "Bitch please, I am a grown ass woman, I do what the fuck I want."

"Chica you trying to convince me or yourself?" Peaches said, "Jay is so insecure before he let you enjoy yourself, he would rather kill you, shit is sad Chica and you know it's true." Deep inside I knew she was right and as bad as I wanted to leave him for being this way Jay was really a good dude. I knew she was right, I also knew the chances of me going was a close to me hitting the lotto in my hood deli, unless I sucked Jay dick rode it from the back bounced up and down suck it again then inhaled his nut would be the only way I could go out and even then, he would blow my phone up.

I wondered off in deep thoughts if I disobeyed him and just went, he would beat my ass and I was scared shitless and I was a tough bitch but Jay took my heart and showed me he was in control of my life like Debo from

Friday. Truth though, Jay was locked up. He been in Sci Correctional Facility for months but I wasn't ready to speak on it just yet. Everything wasn't to tell everybody that's just how people found things to talk about. "Hello earth to Chica." Peaches snapped her fingers in front of my face, "Oh my bad girl." Chica said. I just changed the subject. "Let's hit the mall. Time for us to get these come fuck us outfits?" Peaches laughed and she said, "Google facts."

# Chapter 3

"Candy have you seen my fucking charger?" Low her husband asked while she was laying in the bed trying to relax. Low was damn near 15 years younger than her, he was a cutie for real but he was just way too young for her but she loved him and nothing could change that.

"No, daddy why would I see your charger." she said. "My nigga I left it on the table in the kitchen." She tried nicely to say no, because she knew that at any moment he would flip out and she was not in the mood. She also knew he knows she is going out today, so he feels it's time to start his drama so she can't go. "Daddy I said I didn't see it. I did not even go in the kitchen since last night." "Yo, ask one of your kids if they got it, omg!" "Why can't you just ask them I'm trying to sleep you making a big deal over a damn charger baby please just use mines damn." "No, I want my shit, wow!" "Are you really about to make a big deal over a charger." "What the fuck you mean it's mines if I put my shit down it should still be there. Every time I turn around my shit missing." Low barked. 'Ring, ring' her cell went off, thank goodness cause this nigga bout to piss me all the way off she thought.

"Hello", she yelled into the phone. "What is wrong with you?" Reyna asked, "Girl, this motherfucker got me fucked up." "Oh boy, why I knew it had to be Low young ass." I couldn't stand his ass. He was young, cute, had a little bank and was always on her back; like damn can she breathe bro. See me, it wasn't about me being comfortable I just gave it to her real, she knows in her heart. I'm never a hater I just call it how I see it as she would do me. I had also kept myself in some dumb ass situations. I didn't understand how the fuck she was in this situation. We do 'em dirty we don't get done dirty but she was my sister plain and simple but that nigga needed to go, dead ass.

"What he do now fucking stalker," I asked shaking my head. "Reyna, he flipping over a damn bum ass charger the fuck, sis I'm so tired of this shit." Candy yelled into the phone. She was beyond pissed, "Are you fucking kidding me," Reyna said. "My nigga fuck' him. What time you pulling up?" Reyna asked trying to redirect her mind so this shit didn't get blown out of context. "We got a show to attend where there is going be some bomb ass niggas and if it is the first thing I do I am going to make sure you find a real nigga cause he got to go, dead ass my nigga like he beefing over a fucking charger my nigga. Bitch I know you're pregnant but you still need some fresh air and at least get to look at some eye-Candy, so just don't say shit get your butt up and just please find his damn charger so we can bounce and have a good day." "Nah fuck that Rey, he doing that so he can have a reason to go out and be with one of his side hoes," Candy said "but sis he doesn't have to do none of this he can just go. I have giving him plenty of chances I know he doing me dirty but the tables will soon turn." Guess what we both yelled "Do 'em dirty bitch."

"He is only here due to circumstances, I cannot and will not take this shit no more. I have loved him from the start Rey, all he does is put his hands on me, try and control me, I cannot have no friends." Candy cried. "Don't cry sis, you know you can do better he is a fucking clown."

I yelled, "I hate the way he does you Candy you really need to reconsider this marriage." "Get the fuck off the phone." he barked in the background she didn't respond. "I guess you're going to act like you don't hear him Candy and you know what's that going to do, piss him off, so please get off the phone." "Yup but he will be fine." Candy replied. She kept ignoring him, I knew what was coming next, she still ignored him hoping this one time he would just let it go. "Get off me, get off me my nigga just leave>" she yelled.

"What the fuck, I'm sick in tired of this," I tried yelling at her, "Just hang up?" cause she herself sometimes pushes his button. But of course, now they are going at it. "I have been down for you all these years and all you do is cause pain." 'Click' line went dead because he snatched her phone, I said out loud to myself I knew she wouldn't be going with us. Low took her phone slammed the phone to the floor stepping on it cracking the screen. "I hate you!" she yelled trying to leave the house. He grabbed her turning her around to face him putting his hands around her neck chocking her till she could barely breathe. He whispered, "Bitch I will kill you, do not play with me what the fuck I tell you about telling these bitches our business they just mad cause nobody loves them," he squeezed tighter. She was trying to breathe and at this point she is so scared she just stood there crying silently. "I am sorry." she said in a low tone as pee trickled feely out of her pussy.

He realized she peed and let her go, "Go take a shower you nasty bitch and do not think you going to that show that shit dead, fuck you want to go to a show where there is going to be mad niggas trying to fuck hoes and hoes looking to fuck for a buck. So, tell me why you want to go again." Instead of creating a bigger issue she hurried and went in the bathroom to shower just to stop the abuse verbally and physically he was in rage yelling.

"So you want to get done dirty huh," she rushed to the bathroom hoping it would stop. Well, she was wrong because as soon as she got in the shower he came and pulled the shower curtain back and got in. "Hoe, I am going treat you how you was about to be treated had you went to that show, now turn around put that ass in the fucking air and hands on the wall," she knew what was coming next, he was going to shove his 10inch dick in her asshole. "Arrgghh!" she screamed. as usual he pumped harder and harder till she was bleeding like she was shot, then he pulls his dick out turn around and yelled at her "Suck this bloody dick and you better swallow it." If not, boy would it be hell to pay if she didn't get all of it. she promised she would make him pay! Doing him dirty was a fucking under statement she said in her head as he grunted from her swallowing his cum till there was nothing left. Then he got out and said she had 2 mins to get out and cook. When he got out, she cried "I am pregnant with his son and all he does is do me dirty," vengeance was on her mind. No, he never actually used his fist on her and she had her share of assaults on him but he really just did the most it was time to show him what she is really made of yet somehow, she is in love with him through this disaster marriage they have.

Some days, even months they are great then out of nowhere they seem to become strangers they are at each other throats like they have had some kind of beef in the streets or like she killed his mom. She does not understand it he showers her with so many gifts it's really weird, however she has to give him a scared straight tactic so he will know that losing her isn't in his best interest.

Right now, she just has to think and play her hands. He has no care in the world if he knew she was planning on really living he would kill her also try and harm anyone she held close to her. She couldn't understand why he wouldn't just follow out on his threats.

At this point to die wouldn't be so bad she is so fed up with this drama lifestyle that her heart isn't even really pumping. Now one has a clue everyone except my life is great. Only if they fucking knew she would rather be fucking dead.

# Chapter 4

"Hello." I was in rage as I called Chica, "Yea was sup Reyna?" Chica replied answering her phone, she was annoyed after having a heated phone conversation with her man Jay. "Damn, why you sound like the world just ended?" Reyna asked. "Nah nothing, I'm good, what's up?" she said because she did not want to even talk about it. She and Jay had been going at it for the past two days because she hasn't been upstate to see him in over a month and she slipped up and got pregnant, no one knew which was causing a lot of stress on her she was on her way to the abortion clinic. This was her first time getting pregnant and she really wanted to bare her child but he was a John and the condom broke, shit to be for real she didn't know who the baby was by.

So, the best thing to do was get rid of it, she was getting sick and if she didn't hurry up, she would have a child with no father and no mom because Jay would have killed her. "Are you sure…" Reyna asked, "…because I can call you back if you want or we can go on a killing spree." she said and that loosened Chica up and they both burst out into laugher. "Nah I'm good girl Jay just getting on my damn nerves, you know how that goes." "Oh, no the hell I don't bitch I'm single." she laughed. "But anyway, why this nigga low picking a fight with Candy?" Reyna barked into the phone. "I swear I don't know why she don't leave his ass, he only doing that shit so she won't go out because he knows as soon as she gets dressed and go out mad nigga going to be hollering at her and she gone fuck around and leave his whack ass…" she continued to rant and rave. "He knows that even with that belly she stills going to bag another dude because she is beautiful." "Reyna, Reyna!" Chica yelled till she shut the fuck up, "Dang girl I know you hate him but that's her life. She will leave when she good and tired it's nothing you, me or anybody can do. She will know when enough is enough and trust me she almost there boo. I see it happening sooner than you think, so relax you know this is normal for those two Rey." Chica said. "And trust me, I don't like him nether but she has to figure out what's best for her, not me nor you; so what you need to do Rey is stop getting worked up because she isn't leaving him on our time only hers. It is no need to call her cause nine times out of ten she not going to even answer and then we call her tomorrow she all back in love with the nigga, just stay out of it. So, besides that what time we linking?" Chica asked.

Reyna didn't even hear her because all she could think about was how this nigga don't respect Candy. He fuck with mad bitches. She has proof and still believe him, shit he even tried to fuck Reyna once. Reyna told Candy but she got mad at her and put Reyna out her crib. That shit crushed Reyna so bad, but they are sisters. They stopped talking for a while but like glue they were stuck, so they got over their non-sense. She swear the first chance she get she was getting her a nigga who can fuck and suck her crazy cause that's all he does for her. The nigga always get paid and comes home mad late knowing she doesn't have no money, cigarettes, nor foods; like ughh I hate this nigga. "Hello, bitch!" Chica yelled because Rey became quiet because she was all into her thoughts and checking her DM from this cat from out of town.

"Oh, my bad." she laughed. "I was reading this text from this nigga I met on Instagram." they both laughed. "Here you go fucking with these Instagram niggas.' "Chica I swear niggas on the Gram can suck some pussy you should let a nigga suck your pussy and you'll see how fast you'll leave that nigga Jay." she said meaning every word. Chica looked at the phone and just shook her head Reyna just never let up, but she loved her some Reyna. She was the sister she never had; she did have a sister but have never met her because she didn't want to meet Chica because they came from different mothers. She just wanted to ask her why she didn't want to give her a chance, regardless of whatever, they still shared the same father even though he was deceased. "Look bitch, I will call you back when I pull out my driveway bye, bitch." was the last thing she said and she ended the call. Chica had gotten in her bag that fast and today that wasn't on the agenda. She was on her way to do something she would regret for the rest of her life; as tears fall from her eyes as she stood up and looked in the mirror and decided she would go another day.

All she wanted to do was have a good time, plus catch a good nigga where she can come up off some bank; bills was due and her bank roll was on low. Of course, she had all the bill money but she needed to have ten stacks for play money. That wasn't even enough for a shopping spree her bags cost about eight stacks. Before she could even get in the shower Peaches called. "Hello, yea girl it's no need to go to the mall I actually have a few items I copped last week and their all legit and I know you keep tags on shit in your closet." she laughed. "Alright, now let me get my behind in this shower I have a few errands to run before I pull up on you." 'Heard." she said. Chica laughed Peaches was her girl; she loved her so freaking much but boy was she cheap.

Meanwhile back at home Candy sits in her bed wondering why she allows Low to treat her with so much disrespect and heartache, she knows she is beautiful yet she is so scared to leave. He is my heart she says to herself while rubbing her stomach, her emotions was all over the place. She closed her eyes praying for better days but deep down inside she knows it is only going to get worse. They have been married almost a year and already she wants a divorce.

She has loved Low since the day she met him when she moved into that hood, she just knew he was the one. She was walking with her homegirl on a late-night. "Hey, miss…" one of the little niggas said approaching her, he wasn't for her but she and her girl talked to him and his friend, they was laughing at these two boys, yes boys they was trying to come on strong yet they failed. Another dude came walking up to the two guys with a dog and Candy froze because she was scared of dogs. "Damn that's a sweetheart…" her homegirl said to the guy, he looked up and said thank you. While the dog sniffed her, she was scared shitless she played a lot of games but dogs wasn't one of them, however the sight before her had her stuck. He was caramel with a buffed chest and a red Polo shirt on with some black True Religion jeans and some red in black J's. Yet she wasn't getting the attention she was used to, so she said to him, "You are fine as hell." Yet he didn't reply so her and her girl walked off. "Damn girl he is fine as shit." Candy said to her friend Nay. "Yea, but he must think he all that, fuck him." Nay said.

"Nah fuck that I'm going back I want him." "Candy look at him, he got on mad chains and sexy, yet he wasn't paying you know mine just let him go. "Bitch I'm going back I want him so I'm going to get him, so you're either going to come or get left. I make my own choices." Candy said and she turned around and headed back in the direction of the mystery guy. "Really?" Nay said u-turning she was so mad but Candy could care less all she wanted was to catch up to him before she missed her chance. As she got closer to him, he started walking off, "Damn it!" she said out loud. He was moving fast. Fuck, he had crossed the street but the good thing is he is heading towards my crib. As they walked, Nay was still pitching a fit.

"What am I going to do?" she asked Nay. "Excuse me," Nay called out and with luck he turned around, "Can you slow down my friend wants to talk to you." It was dark yet he slowed down and that's when it all began Candy and Low became one. She laughed out loud thinking about those good days. There was a time he was the best thing she ever had, now he is this monster. She cannot stand the way he treats her after all the times she held him down when he ran low and didn't have a job, and now he just shits on her. He makes good money and he hands her $50 sometimes he will give her $10 dollars. She does know sometimes he doesn't work a lot of hours, so sometimes she think she be over doing it and giving him such a hard time. It hurts like hell because she really sits back and waits for him to love her again, knowing he will not and that he doesn't love her now.

It is just confusing at times because he really can bring out the best in her she thought. He has the ability to give her so much life yet hopes of being dead too, she thought as she looked at him as he slept with not one care in the world; while she is there crying herself to sleep wanting to hold him because he will not hold her. He especially gets mad at her every time she attempts to hold him, he always shoves her off of him. They have so many fights then he will leave and then go stay with his sister. She doesn't like Candy at all because she thinks Candy is too old for her brother. This bitch always letting him fuck her friends shaking her head only if she knew her ass is on my list as well. My girl Kiesha is going to rock that ass and she will never see that ass whopping coming ever, then I am going to have the last laugh. Actually, I promise I am going to bring that whole family down without even lifting a finger. This relationship has ran its course soon as her son is born, she was leaving him, she was just saving her bread so when she leaves she will have enough bread to make sure her son has everything he needs till she can get a job.

It may take her a little longer to leave but Low will be so surprised he will be ready to fucking kill her. She wasn't leaving to hurt her child nor keep him from his father because she knows through all their drama, he will be a good father. He wants to prove to his dad how he should have been a dad to him. She was going to let their son know that leaving his father was not to have him fatherless. She had to save herself from him because he was a threat to her and she knew he would never hurt their child but she was just scared.

He would hit her while he was in her stomach, force her to have sex with him even when she didn't want to. When she was sick and throwing up, he still made her have sex. This man just violated her every chance he got, he finally had a stable job and he is staying with his sister. He said he felt free and that's what's best for him. She knew that wouldn't last because in his heart he knew she was as bad as they come.

She didn't have any problem getting another man. I am out, so since he can look me, his wife in the face and tell me he is thinking about finding someone and settling down with them but he first has to make sure she is stable. "So are you seeing someone yet?" she asked him. "Nah I just be liking pics and shit nothing too crazy." he replied, I laughed thinking about his disrespectfulness. 'Me and my son is out' she thought. Soon as he is born, I will have the last laugh.

Now enough of this pain in my heart let me get up and get me something to eat. this little boy is hungry he is kicking like crazy, 'mommy feed me'. The thought of me knowing in almost 3 weeks I am about to meet little Low; I wonder what he is going to look like. Will it be me my kids or this clown ass nigga Low cause all we do is fight. As crazy as it seems he will be a junior though.

Hmmm chicken zucchini seems like a plan with some white rice with brocciu and cheese and a cold Pepsi, yea that will do. Shit, I know my girls are tight they know me wobbling and fighting with this nigga I wasn't going nowhere. I know they hated him but I move at my own pace not theirs and no one else.

# Chapter 5

"Hello." Chica said into the phone. Peaches shouted, "About damn time. I am coming down now." Click, Chica was mad as hell that Reyna had told her to come and get her but she wasn't even home. Chica thought she would be waiting. See Reyna was from Webster dirty ass projects and lived on the 17th floor. There was no fucking way Chica was parking her candy red drop top convertible in no projects. Her doors had butterfly wings, her rims were chromed out, so she knew her shit would most defiantly get stripped or stolen. Nope, she refused to park her baby there. That was the reason it took so long to get to Peaches. Peaches was going to give that Reyna a piece of her mind. She played games, however, wasting her gas wasn't one.

Thinking about the first time her and Reyna linked up in the town. Reyna had beef and called her but she had missed the call due to her being in the shower. She then saw a text message. It read the 'ops trying form on the kid crew up meet me now'.

Reyna is about 5 feet and 7 inches; baby girl has more curves than the curves on the street. She has honey complexion and she has hair down her fucking back like she is mixed with something. However, she isn't mixed. She is straight up black and has been living in these dirty ass projects with her crackhead father and her dope fiend mother. If she hadn't met Peaches in prison and if she wasn't so cool and real, she wouldn't be caught dead with her. Chica is fly as hell and so gangster, however shorty is down to always catch wreckage with Chica with no questions asked. She felt so close to her that she got out of prison after doing 5 long damn years that she promised her after she was released, she would keep in touch. And that is what she did because she was built that way and the rest is history.

"Chicaaaaaa!" Peaches sang jumping in Chica shit. Why your fake tuff ass never has on no music when you pull up?" She teased, "Let me find out Chica isn't as tuff as she portrays. Put my shit on. You know I need to hear my shit." Putting on 'Pull Up' by Cardi B, Chica laughed and just shook her head at the chicks who fake pumped on Reyna when the gang came sliding through. The song 'Pull Up' by Cardi B pumped through the speakers and had all heads turning. Next you heard doors slamming and they immediately went to popping off on those bitches no questions asked. Then after that she made that her theme song or she would play 'Beef Foreva' also by Cardi B since they beat them bitches asses over there about a month ago.

Shorty be acting like she still wanted the drama, so they beat them hoes again. Now Shorty lay low cause baby girl Reyna had taken away all Shorty street cred in front of the whole hood. Her friends always outside, so this the shit she played picking up her girls to send a clear message that she is a gangster bitch. They pulled off with their middle fingers in the air where ever they are.

"You heard from Candy since we last spoke?" Peaches asked. She shook her head nope, "You know Low broke her phone most likely, so she isn't going to answer no phone. I am assuming cause every time I called her shit keep going to voice mail. She will call sooner or later. You know Low probably up her ass now trying to be all nice in shit." "Damn she stupid she falls for his lame ass every time. Any way you ready to be a thot?" she asked Chica. "Bitch I ain't never stopped da fuck." she laughed meaning every word. "How you think my bank account stay heavy and my insurance is paid on time?" They both laughed. "Okkkk, Chica for real I really need to get out theses damn projects for I permanently take a bitch out of commission." she said looking off into space thinking about her life.

"I got brains, the body, but working a nine to five isn't for me." Chica laughed "Bitch that's not for me either. Chica you got a gift bitch. You can talk a nigga out his snatch really quick." "See me Reyna, I ain't got no time to convince no nigga to give me money you want this ass I want some cash and real cash I need a band. And that is just for an hour bitch, I'll do three at one time to get that bag. I am taking it in every hole for and extra hour for all three; that's another 3 bands. Fuck it, I had been on this road for a long time. Thanking God, I never caught a disease. You feel me? This is my income sis, 10 bands a day for about 3 and a half hours." Peaches laughed. "Bitch what you trying to do because I got the body and I am going to use it till I am old as dirt. I am not going to lose my house to be on public assistant working for no fucking $9 an hour after taxes. I would not even be able to pay my phone bill. Then I'm going to have to find a second job just to stay afloat. Nah, I'll be selling this pussy until I get millions. It's funny cause nigga talks about me bad. Yet, the reality of it is I'm doing 'em dirty every time. You know me, some niggas end up in a fucking body bag if the bank ain't right feel me; I'm not playing with nobody."

"I know what it is like to be on welfare working for food stamps and that little one hundred and forty-five dollars. I am done with that shit." Peaches just listened because she knew Chica was right she just couldn't see herself making hoeing her profession. As they were pulling up Chica told Peaches to call Reyna one more time, but of course there was no answer.

They pulled up on time to catch the show thank God it was outside and the weather was great. They both looked stunning rocking their Fendi capris and their stilettos with ponytails and a Chinese bang. They knew they would crush shit. They always crushed the scene when they made their entrance. They had tried to reach Reyna of course she was nowhere to be found. She was most likely laid up, they decided to park and enjoy the show. It was so many fly ass niggas out there. They giggled a little because they were getting ready to breakup somebody home.

"I'm rolling bitches be strolling," JoJo had the crowd hyped performing his hit single Rolling. Peaches joined in singing the lyrics "...strolling we strolling," as she looked at all the get money niggas around trying to spit game. She wished she could get next to one of them celebrity niggas. As Chica searched for a parking spot she was beginning to get mad. "Shit!" she said out loud to her self-turning to her left. She noticed Peaches stopped singing and was looking at her with her fucking face all screwed up.

"Why you screw facing me bitch?" Chica asked confused, "Look over there, isn't that fucking Reyna over there hugged up with umm that got damn disrespectful ass nigga Kale?"

"Oh, hell no." Chica said as she parked in the middle of the lot. At this point she didn't care. "Girl let's go, she is going to learn one day fucking somebody man. here you go."

"Don't you screw peoples men?" Peaches said. She laughed a little, "Anyway she know his baby momma is a fucking psycho. Sharmaine play a lot of games but not with his bum ass, nobody got time to be beating her ass especially when he doesn't even pay like her anyway."

"Hello." they both said in union to Reyna as they walked up on her. She turned around without moving from in between Kale's legs. "Aayyyee you hear JoJo he killing it." They looked at each other, then to Reyna. "Bitch why the fuck you didn't pick up your phone, we both been calling you?" Chica said grabbing her arm pulling her out of his lap. "Not to fucking mention you had me drive all the fucking way to your spot and don't be there, bitch real inconsiderate."

She seemed to look confused as to what the fuck the problem was. Reyna not knowing she just saved a fucking unstoppable beef. Sharmaine was walking through the crowd of course looking to see who ass was all in Kale face. "Why you all grabbing on me like that girl, I'm finna get that dick and some bank out this nigga tonight?" she said laughing.

As they stepped a few inches away Chica turned her around, "Bitch look." "Look at what, damn?" Reyna said now getting upset thinking she hating. Chica turned her face to the side and look at that crazy ass baby momma of his on the prowl looking for a fight. "He isn't worth it because it doesn't matter if she wins or not, she will not stop till some blood is drawn." She thought about it for a second. "Girl, you right. Shit plus, I look too good to be ruining my new outfit." they laughed.

"Let's bounce, I need a new baller and some new dick and I knew I was going to find it here." Shit that was the reason they came out. "Bitch, I'm not playing with your ass ether, you owe me gas money." Reyna didn't pay Chica no mind so she laughed it off. "Where my bookie Candy pregnant ass at?" she asked. Chica wasn't getting nothing she thought. The two just shrugged they shoulders and headed towards the stage. "Bitch, what niggas we bout to do dirty?" Reyna asked laughing. The girls said, "Nobody is off limits we do 'em dirty babes remember that. I just hope I don't got to kill nobody damn kid tonight, niggas always trying to short change a bitch." Chica said. They all laughed.

The show continued and they watched as all of the somebodies were trying to run game on these week ass hoes. Some shit was really sad the Do 'Em Dirty crew was all bad and all the niggas wanted to get at them. They weren't your average girls, they came with a price a high price. Well mostly Chica, she wasn't sleeping with no nigga under a stack period. The rest wasn't so high maintenance but they don't have as much game as Chica. She was still training them yet she knew they would eventually get to her level. They were her girls and she loved them no matter what they did. Whatever she required from them period they did.

She let them figure life out for themselves her #1 rule was never give up no snatch to no john without getting that bank. they will try and play you every time that's how she sent a couple niggas to their moms in a casket. She was wicked she straight up came reckless. She doesn't have no pops nor a mom the streets raised her. She was so fucking beautiful and her heart was gone; she was heartless and cold like a doubled-up brick of frozen ice.

"Girl is he coming over here?" Chica asked Reyna and Peaches. They both looked ahead at that handsome thang coming towards them laughing "Yup." they both said. It was funny to them because somebody had her by the balls without even knowing it. She was a tuff cookie but it was King's strong demeanor she was afraid of. She knew of King and his background shook the cities. She couldn't get over on him little did she know he was her match. Chica tried to act as if she didn't notice him coming but the anxiousness in her gave it all away. She was blushing from here to the moon. She had been avoiding King for quite some time now. She knew now at this point in time she was caught like a thief in the sky. He was on her. "Hello ladies." he said in his soft voice although he was a straight up in down gangster. King was a ladies man. He was really soft like a baby just being born he wasn't the committing type. He made all the women he dealt with feel special. Kind of crazy because it has got to be something wrong there isn't no way these hoes aren't fighting over him. King got bank, like a fucking real bank. He looks hella good; matter fact he looks damn near better than that nigga

Tyrese. Lord we all know Tyrese looks like a chocolate milked M&M. He stood 5 feet 9 inches and word around town said the dick was long.

"Hello." they all waved smiling from ear to ear except Chica. She just shook her head. Chica was a seller not a buyer, so she tried to stay clear of him at all cost. She never turned down no money but honey she was sure trying to turn down his cause he was just creamy. Women couldn't resist him for shit. he had two women living in a two-family house. He paid all their bills and they didn't speak not a word to each other with one living two houses down. Un-freaking believable she thought looking away.

"All I get is a head nod, not a verbal word to come out those beautiful lips of yours?" he chimed with that soft voice. She shook her head again thinking if he was a regular mark, she'd take all his money. However, King wasn't an average john he was the man every bitch would sell their soul for a chance at him. Nah, he didn't fuck with no passenger side chicks either; all his of chicks was diamond's, honey. I must say that's why for the life of me I couldn't understand why they accepted being side lunch she thought.

"Wad up?" she finally said because like a piece of loose-leaf notebook paper he was putting holes on her.

"That's what I'm tryna figure out because you won't let me get near you. I want to know why." he questions licking his lips. "This chocolate won't melt you." he said with a wide grin. Smiling, she said, "It's not that love, I'm not ready to make you come from the birds nest you're trapped in with your mamma." she said smirking. "Chica, Chica that's real cute." on the inside he wanted to smack her till the sun burned across her face, not one female ever ever talked to him in that manner. Then again that's exactly why he wanted her cause he knew she was scorched on the inside from her past and playing rock was how she protected herself.

Niggas loved Chica even though an hour with her she wanted a band and she made it worth it. Niggas would run trains on her. She had so many tricks up her sleeve that by the time she finished with them they would be in love. so they thought they was getting over but they would lie, steal, and cheat to get the bank to give it to her. She was their hot coco on a blizzard night. No matter what she sold, niggas never told cause the worse part was her snatch was a thousand for an hour. So, she was their treat and they were her trick. As soon as she reached her destination the clock started, so if you choose to do any type of drug before she started to complete her job duties. that's on you which she loved every minute cause all it took was 20 minutes and she was done. She would have you sleeping like a newborn. One nut rule period that's the funny part so if you couldn't hang, she didn't care that wasn't her job to make it last. She would surly finish her job description and leave you there looking stupid. If you got mad and try to violate, she would laugh go change her clothes in the bathroom then kindly pull out her baby blue 22, aim it at your head and pow you quickly loss your life over the pussy.

So, King proceeded with caution because he knew this ice was frozen and it would take some time to defrost. He heard too many stories about niggas not making it out once she was with them. he also knew the whole story too he had sent a few johns her way and found out why she took niggas life and he respected it. If you knew the circumstances and the rules they were to be followed out and some niggas were just fools trying to get over and she just wasn't the type you could get over on. Because she was so strong was one of the reasons he wanted her. He knew she could hold her own he just couldn't understand why she lived that way. She was so flawless she deserved a king like himself to take her and sweep her off her feet. She resisted him all the time, soon as he was in her presence he would turn his back and Chica would be gone in a heartbeat. He wanted to know why she had this wall up so high she wasn't trying to come down.

"Let's say we go somewhere quite to eat and watch the stars till the sun comes up." "Nigga I just told you I am going to leave your ass in yo momma bird nest, cause trust you don't want this here." she said pointing down to her kitty. King laughed real loud, "Lil mamma it seems to me you the one scared to leave yo momma's bird nest. Aww you still not ready to flyyyyy." he laughs. Meanwhile Reyna and Peaches crept off leaving her by herself. She laughed on the inside because she knew what they were up to then. They were tryna to see if she was really as bad as she thought she was because King was no average nigga. He sold game stronger than a basket on a full court.

Peaches and Reyna were all up in these niggers Shocker and Dell's face. She kept her eyes on them because she heard about them and she didn't like them. They were cute with a little bank but they fronted a lot. They weren't really trying to give up real bank they would give $200 bank the most. But you have to do a lot of tricks for that bank. She could get that from just a conversation but she actually didn't mind the conversation because it was starting to get good. King had her laughing hard she really was enjoying his conversation and before you knew it guns shots rang out 'blam, blam, blam' "Oh shit!" everybody ran for cover tryna get low.

Chica tried to run and look for Reyna and Peaches but King snatched her and threw them both to the ground. he wasn't trying to get hit or let a stray bullet hit her neither. As they fell to the ground, she paused. He was laying directly on top of her, their eyes connected and on que he passionately kissed her and even though she loved it, she felt different because she didn't kiss no man passionately besides Jay. She closed her eyes but this wasn't the time. She needed to make sure her girls were fine, she quickly pushed him to the side and screamed "Peachesssss, Reynaaa!" trying to search for a response she didn't hear one. 'Blam' more shots rang out all you could hear were screaming and cars screeching tryna get away… "Just relax we'll find them just let shit calm down." he said. He was protecting her at all cost.

What he didn't know was this was about to be the biggest change of their lives, "Ahhhhhh oh my God!" you could hear screaming. It seems far but yet it was so close. "Noooooo Peachessss, please Peaches wake up." Reyna screamed. "Peaches please…" but it was over Peaches died in Reyna's arms. "Helpppppp me!" she cried while holding her not never wanting to let her go. Shocker and Dell took off running people started to crowd around them; this was about to be talked about forever. INNOCENT GIRL DIES AT CONCERT!.

"Oh my God get off me, what's happening?" Chica yelled fighting to get king off of her. He knew what was happening. He clearly heard Reyna cry, so he got off her without a struggle. Chica followed the soft cries of her good friend Reyna, she didn't want to believe that the cries she heard was from Reyna as she got closer the crowd just slowly opened up for her. It seemed like it took forever getting through the crowd but in reality she was there quicker than her heartbeat. Reyna looked up at Chica "He killed her, he killed her." she cried. She looked at Peaches laying there in Reyna arms and couldn't believe it. She kneeled down in front and just hugged Reyna and Peaches without saying much. She slowly closed Peaches eyes she died with her eyes wide opened from shock you could tell she didn't even see death coming. Those bullets ripped her apart. Chica whispered "Who did this?" so low no one could hear her. Reyna whispered while tears fell from her eyes "Not sure of who but it was a nigga Dell had beef with, he said something as he began opening fire. I couldn't hear him though." she said choking with her eyes full of tears. "Some lame ass nigga, he thought she was Dell baby mom." that's the only thing I heard him say.

What she didn't know was a dude name Rah had put a hit out on Dell and his baby mom. The fact that his hit man just killed the wrong person was the price he was going to have to pay with his life. Rah didn't do well with mistaking identity at all, he didn't pay for no kind of mistake. Now being that another woman was killed and not his intended target, things were about to get real hot. He was going to be on fire once Rah found out. When Rah find out he would have to somehow pay for this woman's funeral cost. But other than that dude was on point and skilled with that 9 Mag.

Chica just held her tightly this city was about to be burned to the ground. Police sirens could be heard coming. The ambulance got to the scene fast as possible but not fast enough to save their sister. Making its way through the crowd, The drug dealers hurried up and cleared it. They knew the fuck boys better known as the narcs would be asking a lot of damn questions. As the ambulance tried to revive her it was a failure and they just covered Peaches lifeless body with a white sheet. Anger filled Chica's heart, she had one agenda and that was to kill everybody associated with these fucking clowns. She meant every word she said in her mind.

It was a shame she died like that she was the most loving woman in the world, literally. She smoked her little weed and drank her little Saint Ides and just chilled she didn't even have any kids to leave behind. Reyna grabbed Chica pulling her, "Sis lets go." Chica shrugged not trying to leave, Reyna whispered "Let's go." "Don't fucking touch me." she barked at Reyna. "You expect me to just fucking leave her here like this. Huh?" she barked "If you want to go, then just go. She is laying here like a piece of garbage." she cried. Reyna tried hard not to snap because Peaches died in her arms so this was a memory she would live with forever. She thought to herself, "Bitch if your ass wasn't all up in this clown face this wouldn't have happened," but the reality of it was they all came to have a good time, so no one was at fault. She just breathed in and out and calmly said "Sis I know you're hurt but taking it out on me isn't going to bring her back. I don't want to leave sis, but it's nothing we can do." she said sniffling while the tears fell freely. What she really wanted to do was smack dog shit out of her for trying to play her like that in front of all these dudes. Chica turned around and pieced her wam, wam, wam. Reyna was so shocked and caught off guard and before she knew it, she was down.

Chica was giving her blows faster than burning smoke. King couldn't take it anymore he watched as his new side piece threw blows after blows on her friend. He knew she was hurt, but hell so were they both and it wasn't expected. He grabbed her so fast, all she knew was that she was in the air kicking and screaming. I am going to "Kill" you bitch. It's your fault. get off me." she continued kicking and screaming while tears poured down her face she wanted to take her anger out on someone she didn't care that it was her friend, somebody had to pay and fast.

Reyna could not believe how this night turned into a bad dream she couldn't escape. As she got up off the ground she was fuming she got up thinking "I knew I should have dragged this bitch for disrespecting me like this but I thought she was my friend more so sister so I spared her. I didn't think this bitch would attack me. Oh, hell no." she thought "This is it, I swear on my life I going to do her dirty. She got me fucked up; no bitch will ever carry me like that. Now all bets are fucking off. It was time for fucking war I am going to show her how to carry someone fucking hoe ass bitch."

She got up from the floor started looking for her Adelyn Rae purse. She needed her phone she had to call Candy her hurt was beyond overrated. "Ughhhhh!" she screamed walking back in forth while Candy's phone rang out over and over till it went to voicemail. She ended the call and called again all she kept getting was voicemail. "What the fuck! she yelled because she now realized Candy had no phone. So, she couldn't reach her; More anger filled her cause the thought of Low breaking Candy's phone she wasn't able to tell her all the fuck shit that just took place and the truth of it all, she met Chica in jail but she really couldn't stand her whack ass.

Peaches and Candy were her heart, after Chica fucked her man Dice and still till this fucking day Chica doesn't no she knows, that was just a pill she swallowed cause Chica was a seller and Dice was a buyer point blank. What Chica didn't know was she had saw the footage Dice had recorded her slut ass in the hotel room. He went there an hour before picking her stupid ass up and paid for the room went up and set the room up with hidden cameras in the bathroom and all. That bitch portrayed to be clean and getting a stack for a nut well that's a fucking lie. She went in the bathroom pulled her clothes off her panties was black as shit. She wiped her pussy with a wet napkin not even an adult Scott wipe. I mean Dice smutted this bitch the fuck out and I'm talking bussing all in her face. Then made her suck his dick until he was hard again, she tried to resist but Dice wasn't having it. He wouldn't give a fuck who you were, he wasn't paying no bitch a damn stack for one nut. He told that hoe "You want this bread get on the floor and crawl for it and cry like a cat in heat." The fact that this bitch did it, had his dick rock hard. He laughed wicked because he knew she wasn't as real like she proclaimed.

As soon as she got there to his knees he picked her head up by her ratchet as weave, so he thought and to his surprise it was a fucking wig and the shit came off. He was fucking pisst. "Bitch, all this pussy you selling and you don't get no weave you fucking wig wearing ass hoe." he laughed again this time repeatedly and bark again. "Bitch, now turn around and get on all four, bitch." He rammed all 10 inches in this bitch as she started to scream he grabbed her throat while ramming in the slut asshole. He yelled "Shut up bitch take this dick, you want this stack, right?" he kept ramming and ramming until he was ready to cum, he pulled out turned her around then made her swallow it until his body slowly stopped jerking. He sat down on the bed and threw the bread at her which only consisted of 100 dollars. "Bitches like you will never get a stack from me hoe. You just sat here and fucked me any way possible. I am supposed to be your friends fuckin man. I knew you wasn't shit hoe and my bitch doesn't need no trifling ass females like you around her period. Oh and trust me as soon as I get home I am going to tell her just how trifling your dirty ass really is." She started talking shit, he snatched that 100 dollars he gave her back and put that hoe out naked and tossed her clothes out behind her. "Dumb ass bitch." he barked.

As the door slam, she yelled "She will never believe you!" she cried. She couldn't believe she was just violated in the worse way. Was this her karma for fucking her friends man, she thought and called a cab. This was one time she regretted not driving she never drove her shit for a lick. As she got dressed in the cold, pedestrians watched her while laughing as she waited for her taxi. Dice sent the video to her phone; she yelled "No." She knew her street cred was over if that horrible video got out. She called him begging him not to tell Reyna and that she would do anything as long as he never told anyone or showed the video. His dumb ass fell for it and kept smutting her out for a few months until she had him set up.

This bitch had him killed, Reyna had just found out she was pregnant 2 months along. She was excited, she was about to have his baby. She called Peaches because she wasn't sure if she should keep it or not after she found the video. She had plans on getting at both of them but her girl Peaches told her to play it safe. They would figure out a plan. Yes, she knew he wasn't perfect but he hid all his dog ways and never let any bitch he cheated with disrespect her and she was cool. All men cheat period and hers was no damn different. You just had to pick a nigga and stick with him because everybody came with problems. There is no man perfect not even us as women.

So, one day they were in bed Netflix's in chilling his phone gets a text. He acted as if he didn't hear it so Reyna didn't say nothing. About 10 minutes go by all the liquor he drinks sends him to the bathroom, he gets up but doesn't take his phone as he nominally does so she checked it. It was this corny hoe ass "Come to my house I got some new shit I want to try on that dick." By this time Reyna's blood is boiling. she wanted to kill him and her. She remained calm, she laid back down as if nothing never happened. A few moments later he comes out of the bathroom, goes in the kitchen for some chips and comes back and reaches for his phone. He reads the text then turns to her with a serious face "Baby it's that time, money calls and this is a big lick. I've been waiting for this call all day and kisses her forehead." "Cool go gets that bank I need to go shopping." He laughed, "Right shorty, I got you."

He left, she wait maybe a good 5 minutes and she sprinted up, threw on some Victoria Secrets sweats and a jacket jumped in his brother LG car. This was one time she was happy his brother left his car because she couldn't stand him half the time, especially after he called the cops on her but today she loved LG and she followed his ass. He was so damn thirsty he had no fucking clue she was following him. Plus he is intoxicated, by this time her heart is bleeding out of control, her tears wouldn't stop and on que he drives her straight to this fucking bitch house. She was crying so damn bad she couldn't believe they were both doing her this fuckin dirty.

So she parked in da cut for a good 20 minutes. Now she was so anxious she couldn't take no more, she got out about to go bang down the fucking door to drag this bitch and him out. She instantly froze once she heard two shots, 'blocka blocka' and two more gunshots went off. She saw the fire and just like that she watched his body drop. Her heart stopped and she could see shadows and not just hers, as bad as she wanted to do something she couldn't. So she hurried as fast as possible back to the car and as soon as she got in some guy opened the door rushing out towards a red Maximum. He hit the alarm and popped the trunk. it slides up and he hurried and got some type of bag and rushed back into the house. She was hunched down in the seat, so no one would see her. Tears flooded her eyes. She screamed "Noooo," with her hands covering her face. I'll be damned, her phone rung damn near giving her a heart attack.

She jumped but hurried up and answered, not looking at who the caller id. It was this trifling heifer "Hello." Rey said with a shaky voice. "Hey boo, was sup with yo pregnant ass?" she sung into the phone. Rey was lost for a minute, "Who is this?" she yelled while her voice cracked. "Um hello, it's Chica." then she looked at the phone about to speak but as she looked up there were too men carrying a fucking rug that had Dice's body in it. She hunched down again because a car was approaching. She was so scared the car was going to honk its horn so she hung up quick without a response. She put her phone on vibrate cause like clockwork she called right back. Thank God, the car kept going. "Yea hello," she responded. "My bad girl my phone dropped out my hand was sup wit ya?" she asked. Reyna was fuming but calmly responded "Oh, nothing was seeing what you were trying to get into I'm trying to hang out tonight. I just now made mad bank bitch, drinks on me which your pregnant butt." Rey laugh "Nah, not tonight I am waiting for Dice to pull up. He said he had to handle some business then we were going to chill. So, how about tomorrow, plus he takin too long I am about to call his ass. You know him, he probably somewhere in some bitch face. I swear when I drop this load I am going to Do 'em dirty." they both'd laughed. Even though it was killing her she had to remain calm because she was watching them put her man in the back of the trunk and she was also watching and had the nerve to call her.

After she explained to Candy and Peaches what happened they convinced her that nigga was no good. So, he got done dirty that was his karma for fucking her friend and to let her live because her karma was coming I needed to just hope God let me watch.

Reyna couldn't take no more so she made an excuse to hang up. with all this shit running through her mind she just fell to the floor again my friend was just murdered and I just got my ass beat by this bitch like an elephant on a mouse "Noooo," she cried out. "I swear I am going to do this bitch dirty, she yelled."

A guy who they all know from the neighborhood pulled up late, but by the time he had gotten there it was police everywhere and ambulance everywhere shit was hectic, he wasn't riding dirty so he stayed in the cut.

# Chapter 6

He watched everything unfolded thinking shorty was a friend of his man Low's wife. So he opened up his jack and hit Low number. He called him and put him up on game. "Yo," Low answered the phone. Surprisingly he picked up, it was a 404 number and he surely don't answer strange numbers but something told him to pick up. "Who this?" The caller responded, "Never mind that your wife home girl, just got marked at the show." "What the fuck you said?" Low barked, "Who the fuck is this?" "Bro just get here on Robinson Ave." Low looked at the phone "Aight pulling up no breaks," he hung up the phone with the unknown name caller.

He thought he knew exactly who that was who had just hit his line. He turned around looked at his wife and this was really one time he wanted to just hug and kiss her. He wanted to say sorry he knew this shit was about to destroy her. Low was never so happy that he kept her home from that madness. She was pregnant with his first child and even though he knew he was wrong for how he treated her today, he was still glad he kept her home. He was dealing with so many demons and he took it out on her, and yes, his karma would come and he was ready. However, if his karma would have come today and he would have lost his wife and child he would have died. He knew he was incapable of ever fully being the perfect soulmate she wanted.

After that call he would do right by her and his son he promised his self. He just looked at her sleeping but he so badly wanted to wake her up. He knew that her friends couldn't reach her because he had broken her phone after the madness that had happened earlier between them. But looking at her he knew to wake her up with this bad news wasn't healthy. It could cause preterm labor and that was not something he was going for. He had put her through enough stress that day he thought this shit might drive her to the crazy house, on the 7th floor.

Shit was so bad already, once they had gotten married their life had took a turn for the worse. He knew he was wrong sleeping around with so many women or just selling them dreams. He was getting away with it until them hoes started catching feelings. They were believing all those bullshit stories and then they started reaching out to his wife and even though she spazzed out she never left.

She could have on so many occasions. She was beautiful she could have gotten anyone but she wanted him and he was thankful for her staying until the end. He knew no matter what him and her went through leaving her and seeing some other dude reap the benefits of the woman he turned her into now was off limits, at least that's what he thought. All that reflected on him. He shook his head he couldn't take no more of all the terrible thoughts of how much pain he had caused her. He did something he hadn't done in years, he kissed her forehead softly and whispered I love you.

He then slipped out into the dark night, he quietly closed the house door not wanting to wake his beautiful wife. He knew in just a short few hours he would have to break the horrifying news to her that Peaches was killed. He got onto his porch and backed out the driveway. Candy laid their still and pretended to still be sleep truth of the matter was as soon as his phone rung she was up and she heard him talking; she just didn't hear what the caller was saying on the other end. She knew whatever was said had to be serious because he kissed her forehead. something very rare at this point she was just praying he returned home to her. Fuck, all the fighting she was scared. Knots began forming in her stomach something was terribly wrong. She got up thinking out loud, "God please bring him back. Please…" she began saying out loud.

Soon as he pulled off he called the unknown caller. "Yo," the caller answered on the first ring. "Beloved what's the word?" Low asked. "Man hurry the fuck up, shit wild boy. They still got shorty laid out here on the fucking floor covered up with a fucking sheet."

"Nah, beloved is you fucking serious." "Yeah, the damn coroner still isn't here. This shit nuts and bro that's not even the half…" he said pausing. "What else bro?" he shouted at the caller. "Chica turned on Reyna…" he paused again, Low barked, "Why the fucked you keep stop nigga speak." "Man, she beat shorty ass. She was screaming it was her fault had they not been in them low budget life niggas face, this shit is bugged boy." "What niggas faces?" "I don't know I got here right after the shit happen. I asked around nobody said much but shorty got clipped then niggas started dipping. mad fuck boys started coming. You no niggas don't do the boys in uniform cause niggas be dirty, so as soon as I got that info I hit ya line." "Heard you. So, where they at now nigga?" "Well the chick Reyna still here. She just walking back in fort trying to call someone but she didn't leave shorty side." "So where this broad Chica?" Low asked, "This nigga King snatched shorty off of her kicking and screaming. put her in his car and he took her key tossed them to one of his flunkies and sped off but you could hear her going off." "Alright I'll be there in 5 minutes." Click line went dead.

"Nigga what the fuck just happen?" Shocker and his man Dell said to themselves out loud. They were pasting back in forth in Dells crib. "Nigga he really just tried to end me bro. I know it got something to do with this mock ass dude you heard boy say this for Rah. I cannot believe he had somebody on me like that bro. Glad that boy made it known loud in clear Rah was sending a message. I am going to kill this nigga bro that's on everything this shit isn't going to fly bro." "Facts," shocker replied.

"This nigga killed shorty bro, the fuck boys is going to be all on us about that with all kinds of questions beloved. I am getting low, ain't no way I am about to be dealing with this heat." Dell went on and on. Shocker just stood there shaking his head, this was all too much. All he liked to do was fuck bitches and be fly. There was no way he wanted this type of heat. "Nigga did you hear anything I just said, you standing there looking like a fool in the face!" Dell yelled in rage. "Yea," he responded with a little over a whisper he knew now that shit was most definitely about to get out of control. All he had to do was wait for his niggas

Man and Jab and he wouldn't be in this drama. He knew going with Dell there were possibilities of some hype to pop off, but Man and Jab was nowhere to be found and he needed a ride.

He figured niggas knew Dell was with the shit so he decided against his thought, even though he knew it was word buzzing around town that Dell had his baby moms shake some nigga Rah for some real snatch. I'm talking about 200k and Rah had a bounty on both their heads but Dell was gangster he brushed it off. He claim he had no idea what ole boy was talking about and he wasn't trying to clear shit up. He knew niggas wasn't coming to his side with no drama. He had soldiers on his side shoot first with questions later, it was always on site. Truth is his baby mom and him would line up mad big-time niggas.

Dell couldn't figure out for the life of him how dude knew where to find him at. His mind was going crazy did one of his boy's line him. Nobody was off the radar he knew for quarter of a mill niggas would chop they grandmother for that bread. But he was loyal to all his dogs and pray their loyalty ran deep the same way; until he found out who was the informer everyone was a suspect. Then he thought, nigga this is a fucking show everybody was bound to be on deck.

# Chapter 7

Now Rah was some big-time dude but lame as hell. He was a south Bronx cat playing in the major leagues on the drug side literally with his bro and his pops. They had the whole damn South Bronx on smash everybody knew who they were. They had the cars, the bitches and mad bank. yeah, they played with the big things.

However, Rah was more of the calm one at least that's what they thought. Rah also worked and he never takes the same route so catching him slipping was a hard thing to do. When he walked, he walked light so no one could feel the ground move. It was impossible to feel him. His downfall was women, he loved women everyone knew that.

He was a young cat that had three kids, married but was far from faithful. Every chance he could get some free time from working and the street hustle and his annoying wife off his back, he would slide to the club thinking he was low, it was always niggas lurking. He was too known, so the truth was no matter how low key he thought he was it was always a familiar face lurking.

Whether he saw them or not. They knew trying a face off would lead them to a bad situation so the best way to catch him would be through a bitch. What he didn't know was Dell had put Pasha onto him months ago. Pasha being the goddess she was thought it would be easy, truth was it wasn't; Rah was as smart as a K-9 dog and could sniff out bad vibes from a mile away. She saw how bitches threw themselves at him and he was far from interested. she watched him for months before she made her move he wasn't as easy as she thought. Some days he wouldn't even come out but as soon as he did, she was on him. She knew he liked big girls and she was exactly what he needed.

Everywhere he went she went, she had a different look each time she was close to almost bumping into him. She had to be very careful. She didn't want to make no mistakes when he was somewhere it would take her like an hour before she had gotten to his destination. He was way too smart, it was no way she would fuck up, this was too big of a mark.

She knew his drinks, what time he went to work when he played the block. She knew everything there was to know about Rah she had his schedule down packed. So, she finally made her move and slid in his life with no problems or concerns.

She had done this shit too many times, she was starting to get bored with it. She pulled up in a rented baby blue dropped top coop at the smooth gentleman club in the South Bronx it was time to Do 'Em Dirty and she had no worries. She was from Harlem, she knew she wouldn't run into anybody there, cause those two Boroughs never really got along. She stepped out so confident handing the valet her keys she knew she was the show stopper because she watched the eyes of everyone burn holes through her body.

As she laughed on the inside, she walked straight up to the door, with every step she took it was like a roller coaster it was fast but exciting. The bouncers let her in. No search or anything and the females complained because there was a line around the corner to get in.

Milk was performing and it was almost at the capacity so it was about to be shut down and doors closed. You heard voices of the envious females yelling "Hell nah, who the fuck is this fat bitch looking like a fucking cow in that coat?" she laughed. They had no idea what she had to go threw to get that treatment.

She had to go there several times while her target was off the radar to get close to security. Fuck a selected few of them because she never knew which one would be at the door the night her target was there and it was just no way she was paying or standing in nobodies fucking line. she was a goddess and standing in some fucking line was not happening period. She walked in slowly as if she was the star, men couldn't take their eyes off her. She just walked passed all of them until her eyes fell on her target.

She didn't have to do anything; they led her straight to VIP they already knew her order, straight up two bottles of Red Monkey. She stepped behind the red line and just watched like a hawk in the sea. The DJ played her song 'Money Bags' upon seeing her come in. Like clockwork he shouted her out. She calmly smiled, waved her hand in the air while bowing her head down. She had the crown period. She had to break him off a few times too, but hey when you aim, missing your shot wasn't an option. Yeah, let's welcome your girl Pasha in the building he repeated until all eyes was on her.

Everybody looked around, she just smiled because her plan was working out wonderful. All the attention she wanted, she was getting. Especially, that night she got it. Milk was performing, so she knew Rah was a big fan of Milk and so was she. But Milk was an R&B singer, so she was surprised Rah was into R&B music. Everybody watched her walking wondering who the fuck she was, they had never heard of her. Guessing she was some kind of star for the DJ to shout her out like that. She walked in VIP slowly with a champion glass and two bottles and not a sole next to her.

She sat there drinking her Champaign and was on her phone on Instagram. She was pretending to be handling important business. Truth of it was that was her plan. She needed to pretend to be a producer, so she would have something to intrigue Rah. She knew you had to be about something to get his attention. She acted as if nobody else was around in her own little world. Bingo her target walked up after watching her turn down so many others, including her targets good friend Wolf. No female turned Wolf down. He was handsome and his swag was dangerous.

"Excuse me sweetheart," he said as smooth as possible but she never once looked up. She knew it was Rah but she wasn't no pit-bull in training she was a straight up professional. She had to play this right to the fucking t. He cleared his throat and tried again with a different approach he knew his man Wolf was watching. Shit, they had made a 100-dollar bet Rah couldn't bag her. So, since his first attempt didn't work and he wasn't tryna pay that bank he tried it over again.

"Hello Ms. Lady, are you sitting alone?" he asked. she slowly looked up with a frown and said, "What the hell." she pretended to be mad. "Can a girl just have a fucking moment to herself?"

So, bingo that was a shot he used to get her attention. "Oh, excuse me, I didn't know they allowed girls in this spot, so I truly apologize. I thought only women with class was allowed. Thanks for clearing that up I am about to blow this spot. I don't need no little ass girls around me screaming rape."

"I don't need no charges, I am a hard worker; you girls have to stop being in grown people's atmosphere looking like grown women." he said and turned and proceeded to walk away. He was hoping that would get her attention. She was big, bold and beyond beautiful he really was trying his pimp card.

"Excuse me," she said are you trying to be fucking funny honey. I am a grown ass woman." she barked. Until looking up, she noticed this caramel honey with sparkling with teeth and a smile you can't even get with a Kodak. Her whole-body language changed, she smiled. "Didn't your momma ever teach you how to address a woman because that lame ass excuse me bullshit is for little girls." Then she slowly looked him up and down. She was baffled he had on a pair of Louis Vuitton with some Robin Gears, a fresh white v neck t-shirt, and his neck was covered with all kinds of chains.

He was more than eye-candy. He was about to be for keeps and so she had to hurry up and find a way to keep him there. This was her shot she didn't wanna ruin it by seeming to be so nasty.

"I am sorry for being so rude, I have all these lame guys coming at me I really don't have time. I am here on business I am not interested in none of these guys in here." "Well that's understandable. My name is Rah," he said extending his hand. She politely looked at him then extended hers. "Nice to meet you Rah my name is Shalet." "Huh that's different." he said while kissing her hand gently. She quickly pulled it away. "So, would you like it better if I had a common name of one of your previous women?" she said with a firm look.

Shalet was her scammer name. She had quite few names giving her government name was ah no, no. "Wow! What did I do something wrong?" Rah asked with his eye brows raised. She giggled no, but that's a little too much. "Don't you think. You don't know where my hands been," and laughed. "I mean it wasn't up your booty, was it?" they both shared a laugh. He had a sense of humor. She liked that. She thought 'I am going to have a little fun with him.'

"If I may ask, why you are here alone? Are you expecting someone because I see two bottles and only one glass." he said pointing towards her glass.

"Um, well I was waiting for my client but he canceled at the last minute. So, since I was already here I might as well enjoy it," she said. "Ooh, I know you're mad." he said. "Nah it's too many other artists who want to get to the bag." "So, what is it you do exactly?" he asked kind of intrigued since she said artist. She notices the facial expression a mile away, she just had gotten a checkmate in his books.

"How about you remove the rope come in and have a drink with me," she said. While stopping the waiter as she walked by, Hey can I have another glass, please and ah bottle of Henny," calmly she looked up at Rah who was looking at her now smiling and confused. As to how she knew what he drunk. She winked at him and said, "Why does it seem like a problem, you don't drink Henny?" she calmly asked. "At least you look as if you do. You're looking like you're a Henny type of guy, but also like you are pretty clam." His smile grew big and he stepped into her VIP section and sat next to her and waved to his man who had his hand in the air. He then knew he had won the bet and his boy had to give up that bank. Shit he didn't care that was nothing Wolf laughed waving him off.

Rah sure had his ways with the ladies. Just like that he won that bet he turned around at stared at her. "So, what was that about?" she asked. Noticing the hand movements between him and his unknown name friend. He looked at her and decided to be half honest. "So, we made a bet if you gave me your number, he would have to buy me a basketball court for my next house. Since I already have one in my current backyard." He needed to spice up the bet, so she wouldn't think she was some cheap ass female. He quickly realized she was about something and not looking for a come up off no dude. "Hum, very cute but all I'm worth is a basketball court in your backyard; let's see that's only about $50,000, right?"

She looked at him dead in his sexy china-man eyes. "I wouldn't even walk around with that in my purse," she laughed then opened up her purse which was holding even more than two stacks and pulled out a 100k. "I feel insulted." His eyes grew wider than a cold coke head. "Listen, um Rah you said. So, you must have really thought I was some quick piece of pussy huh or better yet shoplifter type chick." He was really shocked he was plain speechless. She knew she just scored her goal. He didn't know what to say, "So drinks on you, how nice." he said.

"I never have had no shorty bye me no $800 bottle," they both laugh. "I must ask why you are walking around with so much money." She laughed hard at him dead in his face. He was confused at her laughing. "So, how much money do guys carry to the club. I'm a female who gets to it love. I can buy this whole club. But that is besides the point. I was going to give my artist some cash but he never showed. It was a little extra for the show he did and it was a flop."

"So, I decided to put a smile on his face but his loss. Now on to the next." He liked her already, shorty was a record producer and had her own bank. What was more surprising she had brought him an 800-dollar bottle. This one was a winner in his books for sure and he was glad he pulled up on her. And just like that she swindled him. He was about to go dipsy diving head first with a cold-blooded prana. What he didn't know was he would soon regret that decision. She had one thing on her mind that was his money and he was a mark and when it all goes down, he wouldn't believe she did him so dirty.

She wouldn't mind fucking him because he sure was a fine ass dude for sure. "I got the bill sweetie just to let you know she said in a serious tone. I spend that on parking," while winking at him. His wood got hard instantly. He imagined how he would be all up in shorty up something serious.

She had no idea what she was in for; he was so skilled at sex it should have been his profession. He drove bitches crazy the way he would eat pussy and ass for hours before he even fucked. They would be begging him to fuck but sometimes fucking was far from his mind. His satisfaction would be from satisfying women that was his nut after making women squirt over and over until they were shaking like they was having a damn seizure. He would get up and just cut leaving bitches confused as fuck.

Some he would call again and some he wouldn't. He wasn't looking forward to nothing else. He had a wife that was just his fun which was crazy cause he never ate his wife ass and pussy so often. That's why she did 'em dirty. She was fuckin his brother right under his nose; it was the game everybody got done dirty. She knew he was a dog but what he didn't know was it was war after she caught him cheating. All the cards in the deck was re-shuffled. She was going to make sure the cards she got dealt was all spades and she had both jokers it was game time. His fucking over time was soon coming to an end.

Pasha realized this was a piece of cake but the only part about this was it was starting to take too much time. Dell was getting mad annoyed because he was always busy but every chance he got it was spent with her. He also always showed her a nice time brought her all kinds of gifts but he really was trying to stay away from her because he was starting to catch feelings for her. And she was starting to also catch feelings for her target which was something she had never done ever in all her years of doing this.

# Chapter 8

'Boom boom' Reyna continued to bang on Candy door. Thank God the kids wasn't home because they would have freaked out thinking it was da fuck boys. "Shit" she yelled jumping out the bed then instantly a sharp pain shot to her lower stomach. "Ahhhhh," she screamed then another pain shot. They were starting to come every 15 seconds she buckled soon as she got towards the door. Now Reyna is freaking out she is thinking all kinds of shit like Low beating her, while she pregnant. She starts banging 'boom boom' Candy started screaming even louder as she heard the banging. She is crying louder with the thoughts of it really being the fuck boys trying to run up in her spot or tell her something she dreaded on hearing that Low was dead. "Ahh" she screamed again 'boom' the door came flying off the handle Reyna kicked it in. That's how much frustration she had at this point Low was about to feel the raft of her fucking fire.

As she ran in Candy's house, she saw how her friend was laying on the floor rolling around like a damn dog in heat screaming. Reyna ran to her in rage "Are you ok. I am here, I am here. Did he hurt you?" Her vision was blinded she ran towards Candy's room looking for Low with her pistol in hand. Today would be the day he died he was going to be her first victim to do 'em dirty. "Ahhhhhh" Candy kept screaming.

Reyna sprinted back towards Candy an that's when it hit her, her friend was in labor. "Omg, Candy I am so sorry I thought he hurt you." The look in Reyna eyes was full of hurt. Candy could tell something else was wrong. She did not come banging down her door for nothing but at least it wasn't to tell her Low was dead. But right now, she needed to get to a hospital; her water broke in just that instant. "Ahhh Reyna my fucking water just broke." In one quick swipe Reyna picked Candy up took her to the coach gently laying her down. Hold on babe this baby is about to come."

Reyna propped Candy feet up with pillows then her head. "Just breathe baby I got you, I have to go get some warm water, towels and scissors just please breathe ok?" Candy shook her head and Reyna was gone running around looking for everything, she grabbed the water from the sink and as soon as she got back Lil Low was coming out.

Candy screamed "He is coming, omg he is coming." "Candy, I got you. Push, just push," she was starting to panic she didn't want nothing bad to happen to her baby. She hadn't heard from Low since he left. It was blood everywhere and Reyna acted as if she knew what she was doing, but she didn't have no choice her friend was in labor and needed her. "Push baby girl." "Aahhhhh" Little Low head came out. Reyna scream "Da head is out, breathe okay."

"Good, now push as hard as you can. Yea give me one more big push," and just like that she delivered baby Low. She quickly wiped the baby off. cut the cord rapped him and handed him to his mother. Reyna couldn't believe she just delivered Candy's baby. Today would forever be a sad and happy day. They say when a person loses a life a life is born. Candy stared down at Little Low; he was so precious he held her finger as their eyes connected.

Reyna stood there watching as she silently cried Candy looked up at her and whispered, "Thank you boo, so much." Reyna kneeled over her and said, "No problem girl. I got to call the ambulance get you and this beautiful baby to the hospital." Reyna called and they were there in a flash. Candy said, "Call Low please." Reyna said, "Fine." She called him, but no answer. So she left a message, "Low this is Reyna, Candy just had the baby and we are on our way to Montefiore hospital." She didn't want to tell her that he didn't pick up. So she said, "He was on his way," at least for Candy sake she hoped Low checks his messages as fast as he gets them.

What she said next was the heart crusher. "Call Peaches, omg she's is going to freak out her Godson was born." she boosted. Reyna just let the tears flow she didn't know how to tell her that Peaches was murdered and died in her arms. "We're here," the ambulance driver said. Whoa, Reyna was never so happy to arrive at the hospital, that gave her sometime to figure out how she was going to tell her that her sons' Godmother wouldn't no longer be the person she held so dear to her heart.

Just as they rushed Candy in Lil Low in the room big Low came rushing in "Where they at?" as much as she wanted to sock him in the face, she didn't need no more drama that night.

"Low calm down," he was freaking out sweat pouring down his face. She shook him "Their ok. Alright. Candy loss a lot of blood. I delivered your son on yawl couch." He looked up, "What do you mean you delivered him?" he asked confused with his face screwed up. She knew he would act like this; it wasn't personal. She knew how Low was. She dated him back in elementary school.

Candy didn't know and they kept it that way. They both knew it would affect her even though it was over 20 plus years. "Nigga like I said her and the baby is ok." and just at that time the doctor came out and said Little Low was fine. However, Candy needed a blood transfusion, she had lost a lot of blood.

They needed an approval of next to kin and fast if not Candy would die. Low flipped "What do you mean die nigga?" he said grabbing the doctor up by his collar. "If my wife dies you mine as well. Call your family before coming out that damn room fixing you ugly face to say that I won't never see my wife again and say your goodbyes because I promise that it would be your last breath as well. Now go in there in save my fucking wife fucking asshole." "Now security is coming, Low let him go please security is coming this is the last thing she needs right now.

"Low she isn't conscious and when she is she is going to want to see you." she pleaded. He let go as five security guards rushed over. "Do we have a problem doc?" they asked ready to drag Low ass up and down the hospital? They prayed he tried to act tuff, then they would really have a reason to give him a beat down and lock his dumb ass up.

Low looked at the doctor his eyes were colder than a dark bored up room with no lights or any windows. He was terrified. In his mind he said 'kick this motherfucker out lock 'em up and throw away the key' but in his heart, he knew Low would make good on his threat. So he took a deep breathe cleared his throat and said "No officers it's just a misunderstanding. This gentleman is just going to go over to the desk sign the consent form and have a seat in the waiting room till his wife transfusion is done."

Low looked at him smirked and walked off towards the nurse's station to feel out the proper paperwork, whispering "That is what I thought motherfucker." Reyna was so happy that no more drama popped off all she wanted to do was see Candy and Little Low. She asked the doctor "Can we see the baby please." At this point he could care less about Candy or her fucking bastard son. Cause that's exactly what he was about to be, little did they know. They fucked with the wrong motherfucker today.

Meanwhile everything is out of control. Chica couldn't stop crying. King drove them downtown to Spice Waterfront Hotel. It was beautiful, it had a balcony with two chairs and the view was straight of the city that never slept, and right under there bed it was see threw floor with all kind of sea animals.

It was amazing. She had never seen something more beautiful and calming. But as bad as she wished to enjoy this or compliment this hotel her heart was broken in so many pieces that not even crazy glue was strong enough to hold it in place.

"Why King, why did this have to happen?" she kept screaming. He didn't think she wanted an answer actually, no one never really did want an answer when someone dies or gets murdered. So instead of trying to give an answer that wouldn't justify it, because the only answer was always the same it was Gods timing nobody really believed that shit.

So instead he just hugged her tighter and tighter and kissed her forehead as he whispered, "I got you shorty I got you." That was something she hasn't heard a man say since her father was alive. He died when she was a kid. He was in prison her whole life up until she was a teenager. She never got to go to father and daughter day at work because when she was one years old a man raped her sister and he killed him with his bare fucking hands and sat on a park bench and waited for the cops. Mine you, she has never met her sister. This man had to be crazy and once he finally came home the daughter of the man he killed, bodied him.

# Chapter 9

It was a hot summer in 1996, Johnny was released after 13 years and he couldn't believe he was actually home and in the streets. He rubbed his hands together thinking all he wanted was some pussy but that had to wait but his girls was on the list first even though his wife should have come first but truth was he had married her in jail after his second year there. She started off ass his pen pal. He whispered sweet nothings to her and he ended up marrying her just so he could get some overnight passes. The weekend pussy was a must, he had 25 years to life the early release date was not considered until he did at least 15 so he figured this bitch was desperate.

He really didn't think that this young beauty would really accept his proposal knowing how much time he had. What was wrong with this bitch he thought, but who really cared he thought he had 25 years. Shit, head and pussy for all those years, he would be great. He promised Chica and Pasha that they would be his first stop plus, since Chica and Pasha had different mothers and hadn't seen each other in 14 yrs. They were 2 years apart. Chica was younger than Pasha and once her mom Bernie found out about Pasha, she took her child away and he never heard from her again until Bernie found out she had cancer and she was dying. She then reached out to him and from there him and his daughter had been in touch ever since.

Getting them to meet up wasn't a problem because Pasha had been in contact with Chica. Chica's mom brings her all the time however Pasha refuses to want any dealings with her. She wanted to be the only one and if she had anything to do with it, she would make sure it stayed that way. Johnny tried talking to her for years but she wasn't having it and she knew her dad wanted them to link up he talked about they were all they got, well he was totally wrong because Pasha's mom had another daughter who she had giving up for adoption because the father of her sister

Reyna was a crackhead and somehow hooked her mother to the drugs.

Her mother had already giving my mother custody of her and to be honest that was the best thing she could have ever done because my mother Ann loved her unconditional. It was nothing she wouldn't do for her. actually, she would still do anything for her but the sad part was she had never gotten a chance to meet her sister but before her mom gave her up, she took a picture that she still has in her wallet. She was a month old and for some reason she really wanted to find her, so before she let another female come in her life talking about being her sister she needed to find her real sister first; that father stuff doesn't mean nothing to her they had the same mother and it is that simple and she clearly explained that to Johnny over and over, so till then I have done that father daughter stuff on my own time and she just don't want to be there.

"Daddy!" he heard from behind him, knocking him out of his daze. As he turned around Pasha charged him. "Hey baby girl, what you doing here?" he asked. She pushed him, "So oh you aren't happy to see me?" Pasha said faking an attitude trying to walk away. "Aww come here princess." he picked her up swinging her around. "Stop, stop!" she laughed hard. "Ooh now you want me to

stop huh? You too grown for daddy to pick you up huh?"
he tickled and then her momma stepped up and said, "Hi
Johnny," Pasha's mom said even though she was still
beautiful and still had that damn apple behind. She loved
pussy though and it was nothing he could do about it. He
walked up on her, she still had that golden girl glow, her
hair still flowing down her back; she was amazing.

He put his arm around her lower back pulled her
slowly towards him and kissed her ever so slowly and she
didn't flinch or pull back. She knew as well as he did
nothing would ever transpire between them again. He was
the last thing on her mind. She laughed, "That wasn't
supposed to entice me now was it?" they both shared a
laugh. Let's go to breakfast on me." she said. "Daddy here I
got you a phone." she said passing him and iPhone X. He
smiled "Thanks baby just what I needed. Do you mind if I
step to the side? I need to just call my mother and that wife
of mines and my daughter your baby sister." she laughed
wicked. "Dad stop trying to force that tranny on me," "How
do you know what she is Pasha you have never even met
her." She shrugged her shoulders and he stepped off to
make his calls.

He knew getting Pasha to meet her was going to
take some time she was a tough little girl. "Hello honey,"

he said into the phone to his daughter Chica who was so excited she finally was about to get to meet her dad and hopefully her sister. Nothing would ruin this day she waited 13 long years. Unfortunately, she never got that opportunity, her happy day and thought turned into one tragic moment she never would forget. "Hey daddy," she sang into the phone as she turned around and around in the mirror, she wanted to look absolutely stunning this would be the first time she meets her father and sister in person. Those pictures of her dad would never amount to in being right there with him in person and she also gets to meet her big sister she was just too excited.

"Honey daddy is going to see you first thing in the morning I didn't expect your big sister and her mother to surprise me picking me up. So, at the moment we're at breakfast. This is my phone number and right after breakfast, I'm going to parole not sure how long it is going to take but my wife agreed to pick me up from there and take me out I am so sorry. Daddy really loves you. I cannot wait to finally see my baby girl." She just stood there looking in the mirror silently letting her tears flow.

She couldn't understand after waiting thirteen years to meet him and all his promises he pushed her to the side like she didn't even exist she was beyond hurt. He noticed her silence "Baby girl I know your disappointed," he paused and took a deep breathe, "How about this as soon as I am done, I am coming to get you. She chimed with joy "Ok daddy!" she thought 'he does care'. She quickly hung up the phone singing 'daddy is home' boy was she excited. Time started going by faster and faster and she had fallen asleep waiting for him. By the time she had waken up, it was three a.m. and she woke up her mom shaking her, "Mom, mom, did my dad come." "Girl are you crazy no that bastard didn't come. I tried to warn your dumb little behind you would be his last stop now get out of here with your ugly behind." I couldn't understand why my father didn't keep his word.

She slowly walked out her mom room closing the door behind her she went back in her room crying her heart out until she went back to sleep. It had been two weeks and still no show from my father or not one single phone call she would call him at least ten times a day and she would get the same results every time his voicemail, "Hi you know who you hit just leave it there and I got you." So she was sitting on her living room couch bored out of her mine and turned on the channel 12 news and I be damned clear as day the news reporter began talking about a man who was found in an apartment rented out by a Tina McBride but Tina McBride wasn't a real name. Then a few moments later the worst day of her life came crashing down like a Mack truck a picture flashed before her eyes.

She was blinded by the constant flashing of her father picture constantly popping up over and over asking did anyone know this man who was killed execution style he had just been released from prison a few weeks back. They had no clue as to who did this horrible crime but they found no phone all they had was his prison identification that is how they were able to identify him. Pasha and them had already found out moments ago that he was killed. The reporter said he was there for about a week his body was cold. He had his throat slit clean across; they also said he was sleeping during the time someone took his life. Neighbors said there were rumors that he was there with a light skin female who said she was his wife but there were no photos of her no one knew who this woman was neither his mom or his daughter has ever physically met his wife. Her name was Iesha Smith but Smith was his last name she had gotten a fake I.D. When she started going to see him, her real name was Iesha Huggins then five minutes later the news reporter came back on "Hi this is Cookie I would like to give and update about the man who was found dead the finger prints that was found was a female woman who we identified as his wife Iesha Smith whose real maiden name is Iesha Huggins the daughter of Sticks who was killed back over a decade by her husband. We're assuming this horrible death was a strong well planned out revenge for him killing her father. That will be all for now."

# Chapter 10

Walking back in forth with no sense of direction Rah was angry his boy just called him and explained to him that he fucked up and bad. He was enraged, he was confused, he paid him one hundred and fifty thousand dollars up front and he fucked that shit up he thought but his thoughts were interrupted as he heard a car door closed. He peeked out the window and it was the hitman for hire he walked towards the door and opened it. Rah was not the loud type so once he stepped to the side letting the dude in, he closed the door and without a word he turned around and pointed his gun which had a silencer. Dude tried to reason with Rah and he instantly began pleading for his life. "Come on Rah, please man it was and honest fucking mistake please man just hear me out," by this time dude is crying. So before taking his life he decided to listen it was only right he did give him a huge chunk of money.

"Speak…" he said "…because no matter what only God can save you now, so tell me how the fuck I pay you all that bread and you kill an innocent girl." "Ok man, I was talking to my girl Nancy because her and ole girl get their hair and nails done together." "What, wait a minute, so you mean to tell me you running around here like a bitch telling your girl you were about to kill someone?" he yelled "This is fucking insane." He pulled the trigger over and over. It hurled him that he just had to kill this man he grew up with he was his family truth was all family isn't the same. He quickly cleaned the gun off rapped it up dismantled it and stored it in his back pack. He then began to start rolling his man up in the rug he killed him on. Once he was done, he taped each end of the carpet so the body was safely secured.

"Yeah," he said into the phone. "I got some laundry that needs to be cleaned" and he ended the call. Now he opened up his phone and made another call. "Was sup my guy?" he said into the phone to Jab. Now he was his little informer on the Westside, he knew everything, so he knew everything. "So, who was shorty related to that was killed at the concert? I need to have information on her and I am going to need you to come pick up this bread to make sure shorty family burry her right because that wasn't meant for shorty," he said shaking his head. "This nigga fucked up bad." he said. Jab said, "So what you going to do to him because I know you paid that nigga bank and he fucked that cake up it wasn't even fully cooked." he laughed. Rah wasn't laughing and he responded, "Nigga just get here so shorty can be laid to rest the right way." Click line went dead.

Shocker left Dell home with so much running threw his mind. This wasn't something that he wanted any parts of but his man Jab set the whole thing up. He knew that little Ramel was going to fall for the fish he planted on the hook. "Was sup man." Jab said to Shocker. "Nothing man you trying to light one?" Jab said he knew Shocker was a fucking square, so this was going to be a walk in the park. "Yeah man I need a loose one. First my girl got me pressed beloved." Jab laughed. "Nigga, now what all yawl do is fucking fight." "Nah nigga she wants to be hanging out all night with this fat bitch from her junior high school she ran into name Pasha. I barely fucking see her let alone get my dick suck." Jab laughed. Bingo that was his way in to get the info he need because he had saw Pasha and his girl light bright hanging out he just needed to verify it was really her before he went and fucked up that package.

He rubbed his hands together and smiled, "So can I hit that man or what?" Shocker was confused. "Nigga can you hit who?" he was ready to square up thinking Jab was talking about his lady. "Nigga I am talking about your girl's old school friend." he laughed and shocker laughed with him. "Hell yeah nigga maybe you can get this bitch from around my shorty cause for real my girl starting to come home with cake everyday bruh. I don't know what type of fuck shit they got going on but she be talking about she selling got damn horse hair." they both started laughing.

Just like that he found a way to get next to Pasha his man just told him how and he doesn't even know it. "Alright bruh, I am about to cut." he said thinking this shit was to easy. "Alright Duke, hollas at me and what kind of hair your bitch sell?" "A man watch your mouth ok." "Ok but you did call her a bitch first." "Nigga I don't know, they sell it at the hair shop downtown on the plains the one next to the market." Shocker replied. He now knew how to get Ramel to fall victim to his plan. "Yeah." Ramel said into the phone, "My main man was sup with you?" he beamed with joy. "Shit man, just trying to find this bitch." Ramel said.

He was starting to get nervous because his boy gave him the up-front bread to pay for his mom's house and medical bills but he still hasn't delivered his product. "Well I think that I can help you with that." Ramel was in a different mood when he heard. "Nigga don't play with me, what the fuck do you know?" he questioned. "So, if I give you some leading information what are you going to compensate me?" he asked. Ramel knew that Jab was serious. He had no family, he was trying to get it by any means and was a loyal little nigga. "Bruh, I got you with twenty stacks right now what you got for me?" he was desperate. Rah was starting to come down on him hard he thought that because they were family, he wouldn't go so hard but he knew with that type of money shit change and he would for sure kill him. All family aren't the same.

"Alight, check it my man Shocker wifey and the bitch you gunning for work together at that new hair shop that opened last week. Your target is the owner bruh, so go check it out. Once you see my information is real, I want that bread in my account. If you don't got the Ca$h App nigga, download that shit quick and send me my bread." "Now what you need to do is send your girl Nancy over there to get her hair and shit and boom nigga the rest is fully cooked."

Ramel beamed with happiness he couldn't believe how Jab came through with that information. He ended that call and like a detective working triple overtime without any sleep and desperate for some kind of break. He finished his cup of Yak and fled his house. He was on a search as he sped down those long blocks on the crowded streets. He pulled up in an instant and parked directly across the street as if it was scripted, he saw one of his targets. "Yes," he screamed seeing that Jab's information was in deed true and without a thought Jab was his hero. He would now put his plan in motion. He grabbed his phone and opened his Ca$h App and sent Jab that twenty bands as promised. And even though Jab's information was 100% correct, it didn't go as planned because Jab told his girl to become a regular and of course her upgrade was real because of the bank they had gotten from Rah. But it was a disaster waiting to happen

Nancy had it going for a minute until they all started linking up and going to clubs and shit and that's where the down fall came Nancy started forgetting that Pasha was the target and they gotten drunk and this dumb bitch slipped up and told her every fucking thing they had in stored for her and when. She told Pasha how this Friday they were going to kill her and how they were paid for hire by Rah. Pasha laughed it off pretending to be so glad that she befriended her and told her how they could figure out a plan so they can keep the money and make her a partner in the business. She even drew up fake paper work for Nancy to sign being that Nancy never really had nothing; she jumped at the opportunity and they said fuck niggas it is females over everything and at this point she helped Pasha plan her escape and promised to send for her after things cooled down.

She fed Ramel all false information about how she was going to be at the show and what Pasha would have on. Ramel had no idea his woman would deceive him. Boy was he clueless to her scheme and this is where he fucked up his life and it was soon going to come to an end. They would soon take over the streets and do everyone dirty. Ramel questioned Nancy for about an hour about was she sure Pasha was going to be at the show because Rah was beginning to get real impatient with him, yes babe she will be there and so will Dell you just have to trust me. She had already went to the show to see who she could see who looked a lot like their intended target.

They didn't live to far so she slid to the show without being noticed and just like that she saw the girl Peaches and stayed there until Ramel got there even though he was paid to take Dell and Pasha out. Rah wanted Pasha first because she stole his heart Rah wanted Dell to see it and know he was next. When Nancy told Ramel what his target had on and where they were posted up at, he didn't waste no time. He started in their direction only five feet away at started firing non-stop until he cleared out the crowd.

Dell and Shocker was almost frozen they didn't have a clue as to what was happening until Ramel was on cue and he heard him say "That's for Rah bitch," and he turned her over about to empty his clip in her face until she didn't even move once he turned her over that's when he realized he hit up the wrong person and sped off the seen. People was bent behind cars, under this whole thing, he just fucked up royally. As Ramel got in his car he called Nancy asap she didn't answer she was gone and that would be the last time he ever saw her again. She had already taken all the money he had got from Rah and that was that. He banged his hand on the stirring wheel and tried to reach her again but nope this time a recorded operator came on saying the number he reached had been disconnected he was pisst.

He didn't know what was going on. What he did know was once he got home, he was going to choke the life out of that bitch for giving him false information Rah was like his big brother he knew what was about to happen, he just hoped that Rah believed in his heart that they were real brothers and would spare him. What he didn't know was that Rah didn't give a fuck who it was he had to kill him because as fast as Ramel did the hit was as fast a Jab lurking ass called him and explained how he killed the wrong person and explained he was behind it. So now everyone knew he had something to do with it and that means police was going be involved and that's just something he had no time for. So it was time for process of elimination starting with Ramel; he had to go. Everyone had to go even Jab because he was brought for the right price that means he can be brought by anybody so he had to go as well.

Back at the hospital Reyna held Little Low, he was so adorable. His real name was Larry Joseph Jr. He was the first child for Low. He couldn't believe he now had a child and a boy at that, he felt extremely blessed. After holding his little junior he knew his world was about to change. It was time to get his shit together, if not for his self for his junior.

He wanted to grow up with Little Larry teaching him how to play ball, how to be independent, everything flashed in his head; he started playing boldly he said to Reyna, "I am about to go check on Meeker then I going to the crib to get her some clothes and stuff, so I can be here when she wakes up and change her." She said, "Ok I am going to sit here with the baby a little bit more I just pray she comes out of that coma. I don't need nothing else to destroy me. I really cannot take anymore fucking drama." Larry placed his hands on her shoulder and said, "We got this, everything will work itself out." "I sure hope so." she said with a light smile.

She was so exhausted she had been through so much she didn't know if she was coming or going. Larry walked out the nursey and headed towards the room to check on Meeker before he headed out. He was such in a zone, he ran into some dude by not paying attention. "What the fuck," he said looking up at dude. "My man watch where the fuck you going this isn't the time." the guy said with his face screwed the fuck up. His stare was colder than an ice pop.

Larry couldn't understand why Duke looked at him with such evilness besides, he could care less all he was thinking about was checking on his wife and then going home to get her and his son belongings for real. "Nah nigga you should watch where the fuck you walking playa,"

Larry said matching dude stir. Duke laughed, nigga you sure in the right place to play mister tough guy. Larry had to catch his self, his wife was in a coma and now just wasn't the time. He waved his hand in the air and kept his movement in the direction he was going. He was sure he would run into this corny ass dude again. As Low walked in the room his wife was laying their so peacefully, he just wanted her to come back so she can be there with their child. He didn't have any children before now, he may have baby sit his brother and cousin's kids but he was able to give them back. He didn't know the first on how to raise a baby if she didn't pull threw.

He grabbed her hand and said a quiet prayer and kissed her forehead and headed out. He couldn't believe how Peaches was gunned down. She didn't do shit to no one he thought to his self. His baby boy was finally born weighing 7 pounds and 2 ounces he was healthy to be born two weeks early. His wife was in a coma this shit was enough to make a sober nigga do every type of drug in the world to deal with all of this. Low didn't know what bitch to call with so much drama he needed some pussy to hammer out. Some weed too, he laughed and pulled out his phone to call his bitch Vanity she was his low bitch; she did everything he said. She always was prepared she kept the liquor the weed and plenty of condoms.

Yeah that's exactly what I need he laughed to his self she was his little rider, she knew about Meeker soon having the baby and she didn't give a shit. She brought they baby mad shit and she had it all at her house and that's what made Low love her more. She was willing to support him. She didn't complain she was everything Meeker wasn't she mouthed off entirely too much and he hated that about her. Why couldn't she just shut the fuck up sometimes. Truth of it is she only began mouthing off once she realized he wasn't as faithful as she thought. She tried leaving him so many times but he wouldn't let her.

She loved him so much through everything he thought, but him being him he was under way too much stress he needed an outlet it was either killing a nigga or getting some pussy. So, since pussy would keep him out of jail that's what he did. 'Knock knock', but to his surprise the door just opened which was pretty strange Vanity never left her door unlocked she lived in a quiet area a gated community and all but she thought most of the killings happened there because no one expected it. Not her, she knew from watching way too many lifetime movies that in the suburbs was a high rate of murders.

Low closed the door behind him and locked it. He heard slow music playing in the background he smiled to his self he could smell the honey glazed candles burning in the air. it calmed him down from his suspicious thoughts, he thought what the hell is wrong with you man you all paranoid and shit for no reason he chuckled as he walked into the living room where there were two wine glasses on the round table the lights were dimmed there was a bottle of his finest wine on ice she was really amazing. He wished Vanity was his wife but truth was Meeker was. He poured him a glass he sat on her red leather sectional and let the wine go down smoothly there was no reason to warn her he was there; he knew she had known because she was in the shower and the shingles she had connected to her door was loud enough to wake up the dead. He heard the water running he thought maybe a sexual episode in the shower would do him justice hot water running all over his body while he slid his dick in and out her tight vagina would be so peaceful he got up and started taking off his clothes piece by piece and as on cue the music changed, he laughed to his self. Do she got cameras because this song she put on was baby making music and it kicked in, then he u-turned because he needed a condom. he had too many encounters of unprotected sex. One time she actually had gotten pregnant but she promised she would get rid of it and she did. Truth was she was never pregnant she couldn't have kids. She did that as a trap to get him to believe she was an understanding woman and she understood her position.

Nah she had another agenda on her mind she was getting surgery so she could get pregnant she was saving his cum inside her mouth every time she sucked his penis and he ejaculated she would get up spit in a clear cup with a lid but she had to be quick because if the air hit it wasn't no use for it. If he wasn't so damn drunk all the time maybe he would have realized the fuck shit she was doing. She wanted him all to herself and as soon as her plan worked and she got pregnant she would go straight to his wife without two fucks given, he would then see he was done dirty. As he got the condom out of his pocket, he heard the water turn off he rushed to stop her from getting out his lovely vision throwing her against the shower doubled doors, fucking her doggy style real ruff.

Vanity loved the way he fucked her she through that ass back harder than a hard cover science book she knew that's how she would get his baby he never pulled out doggy style she had his ass moaning harder than a constipated nigga. As he reached the bathroom door he called his self-surprising her. He was surprised by seeing her in the bathroom tub with a shot to the head blood was gushing out of her head. "What the fuck!" he yelled he started bugging. How, why, all kinds of shit was running through his head, he was standing their naked and he heard a car door slam that's when it hit him, he ran to the bathroom windows and just like that he saw a guy run in a dark tinted cameo speed off down the streets. "Fuck!" he screamed banging his hand on the window seal.

"How the fuck did I just get set up like this?" he turned and looked at Vanity shaking his head he wondered what the fuck she was doing that he didn't know about. He thought he knew her every move and it is clear that he really didn't, with that he went to run and get dressed and wipe down everything he had touched he couldn't believe this shit and just as he turned around, he saw his name imbedded in blood 'Larry you fucked with the wrong one'. His eyes got real big and instantly closing, he shook his from side to side he looked closer and sure as day there goes his whole name in bold letters. What the fuck was happening. He grabbed a towel and wiped the mirror down and hurried up and got dress this was a fucking nightmare. He threw on his hoodie and crept out closing the door behind him.

As he drove away, he saw about five cop cars flying pass him. It was no way they were going there unless who ever killed her, called the cops was trying to frame him for her murder. Fuck he yelled he didn't get a chance to wipe down shit before he left. Why the fuck is this happening to me. Ring his phone was going off, he wasn't in the mood for no one's bullshit as he looked at the phone it was an unknown number. He sent it to voicemail he didn't answer no type of unknown numbers, no block calls, or any of that shit because it was always a hoe he fucked and avoided calling crying and now wasn't the time but the unknown caller called over and over he finally fucking answered "Yeah who dis?" he barked. The unknown caller responded be careful who you make death wishes on. Next time it will be that beautiful son of yours that was just born. Then the caller hung up. Low was in rage who the fuck was that he called Reyna phone she picked up on the first ring, "Damn nigga where you at you sure is taking a long time. I'm hungry." "Where you at?" he barked. "I'm at the hospital nigga. Are you ok? she questioned sensing something was wrong. "Nah nothing." he said. "How's Candy?" he asked. "Well, she is still the same, I'm sitting here with her just praying she pulls threw." "Alright, well go in there and sit with my little man. I'm on my way." "Nigga bring me

some damn food please. I haven't eaten shit all day."
"Alright, I got you." and he hung up.

Low felt a little better knowing his son was alright but he was about to be fucking this city up; someone was threating his son who's only a couple hours old. Hell nah he wasn't going for that, too many niggas hated on him so it was no way to narrow down his search but everyone he was beefing with was about to have someone they love to disappear to make a statement. As Reyna headed down the hallway to check on little man she stopped at the vending machine and got a bag of chips and a soda and also noticed a cute guy coming her way and she stood there a little longer. She needed someone to clear her mind after all of this. As if he was reading her mind, he approached her smiling, "Hello beautiful," she returned his smile "Hello." she said waving. "So, I've seen you here for a few hours who you here with?" he questioned. "Oh so how was it you seen me and I didn't see you? Are you stalking me?" she said, "Ha ha." he laughed. "Nope as fine as you are, I should be." she instantly wanted him he was turning her on. "As fine as you are there is no way that if I was your man I would let you out of my sight." "So, what's your name?" she asked him. "Finally, we're getting somewhere." he said. "Well since you insisted my name is André." "Ok,

nice name." she said. "Oh that's it I don't get your name?"
he quizzed. She smiled slightly "My name is Reyna."
"Hum that's a very pretty name." "Well thank you sir, well
let me get my food so I can go check on my nephew." "So,
where you going to get your food from?" he joked. "I sure
hope you're not talking about this junk right here are you?"
"Well yes, I am if you don't mind it was nice meeting you."

 "I hear a baby crying, I have to make sure it's not
my nephew." "Ok, I'll see you around." His mission was
completed. He needed to stall her long enough to get the
baby out of the hospital. He smiled, he was going to fuck
her bitches. She is so damn retarded he thought. He
proceeded to the elevator as if he didn't have a care in the
world he could care less about bitches, he just wanted to
fuck and that was that. Reyna was now on his list of bitches
to fuck. She would need someone shoulder to learn on after
what she was about to experience. He laughed that was and
easy score. As he got off the elevator Low was getting on
it. Low thought to himself 'that was the same guy who he
had bumped into earlier.' Duke said, "Was sup homie you
looking like it's a problem." Low grabbed him up so fast
and put the gun to his head "Nigga do we have a fucking
problem cause this is the second fucking time I saw you
and you keep trying me so was sup bruh? Oh now you quiet

nigga huh? I am not to be fucked with, so let's make this shit here clear don't create a problem if it isn't one because I'm with anything you want to do." Duke threw his hands up in the air and just that fast the alarm's started going off Low went into a panic thinking it was his wife and got back on the elevator and press the eight-floor "Nigga you just got saved by the bell you bitch ass motherfucker." As the doors opened, he rushed out and his heart damn near stopped there were cops and nurses everywhere.

Once again, Reyna was screaming to the top of her lunges "Where is he?" she had attacked a nurse because as soon as she had gotten to the nursey the baby was gone so she waited for a few before she questioned where he was. She had thought they took him out for blood work and at that point the nurse knew there was a problem. She questioned a few other nurses who was on duty no one had a clue. She was so hysterical that the police was holding her down. "Low!" she yelled "someone took the baby, he's been kidnapped." Low started wilding, he knocked a couple cops out he became so outraged that they had to taze him. They didn't want to hurt him they knew he was angered because his son was just kidnapped but he needed to calm down. Now there they both where handcuffed not under arrest but just so they could question them because a baby doesn't just disappear out of a hospital with no witnesses. "This is about to be crazy press." the police officer said to his partner and to make matters worse, the nurses came over the intercom "Code blue, code blue!" all the doctors ran in the room. Candy went into a deeper coma "Noooooooooo" Reyna yelled as she saw them running into Meeker room. "What the fuck is happening?" she screamed. All Low could do was fall to the floor. "Why is this happening?" he started going crazy. "What is wrong with my fucking wife? What's wrong with her?" and in a flash the same doctor from earlier came out and looked at Reyna then Low, he said, "I'm sorry." and walked away. Low screamed "I'm going to kill you." This shit was fucking unbelievable how can this all happen in the same day

# Chapter 11

"Yo," Rah answered into the phone "Open up big time I'm outside bro." Jab said and ended the call. He was all too happy because his plan worked out great. As he walked into Rah crib he immediately notice the rug gone he played it cool though he knows better letting Rah know he notices so much. This mistake could be his biggest down fall ever. "So, what's the word?" Rah asked him. Jab instantly began giving him the information about Peaches and where she was from. "She was a Harlem girl and she ended up moving to the dirty ass Bronx. She was a good girl hanging with the wrong crowd and by being at the right place at the wrong time hanging with the wrong niggas her life was cut short." Rah just listened because Jab didn't miss a beat he was going in for the kill, so thirsty he told on his damn self not even realizing sometimes it is just best to answer what your asked period no long drawn out story exactly what he did.

Rah said "You is a fool." shaking his head, If he can slip up like that and don't notice. Ain't no telling who knew what was really going on but Rah already knows the truth. Ramel already had told him everything so Jab's death was near; all he did was help him much faster. "Alright, so did you speak to any of shorty family?" Rah asked even though he already had all the info. He just needed Jab to feel more comfortable because his guy LG was on his way, he would rock poor Jab right to sleep; he was like a dog who turned on his owner for a piece of steak. Disloyal, he was about to meet his man in hell.

Right on que, LG came slow strolling in Rah's house. Jab knew who he was, so he really didn't think twice or sense no fear. He knew Rah loved him like a little brother LG really wasn't friendly. He never spoke verbally to anybody he was scary, he always wore a hoodie no one really ever saw his face because under his hoodie he kept his hat low covering his eyes with his box braids in his face and that thang safely stashed in his holster connected to his ankle nobody would ever see there death. He was quick, quiet and he would be gone as fast as you saw lightning.

He didn't like deceitful people, he didn't care if you were his family or not, he would make you clear as a strip on a roll of tape trying to see it was hard because it wasn't a line, you'd have to create one. "My main man LG what's good bro?" Rah said tossing him a roll up, he needed to get tossed up it was so much shit going on his head was spinning. "So, bro what happened at the show?" LG asked Jab he looked at Rah he was confused because this would be the first time Jab would actually have a conversation with him. "Nigga fuck is you looking at me for, cat got your tongue?" "You should be answering, you know he don't rock with nigga. You should be lucky he even talking to your little ass, shit I am actually shocked." he said laughing. Nigga, you alright?" Rah asked LG. "Nigga I know your ass wasn't at the show, so I am talking to the plug and it is not you." By now they are all laughing and just like that LG wheeled him in and before sunrise he will be joining all the dead homies.

Jab just knew things were looking up for him and he came up off Ramel and he knew Rah was about to bless him with some doe as always. Plus, the bread for shorty funeral and her peeps, they would only get half of that. He laughed to himself he was about to really come up and as soon as he was done, he would go to the precinct and give the boys the information they needed to get Rah and he would soon take over. With Rah out the way Dell on the run he would be the next big thing. The cops would be off his back for them guns he got caught with and with all the people he got pinched Rah was the last one because he wasn't the big fish, they wanted his family. They couldn't get near them though, now with Jab being able to bring him right to them, they would get his whole damn family. But they would be destroyed once their informant came up missing and they had nothing.

Jab was so excited to go get that bread plus, Rah confession he forgot his Rolex watch which had the recorder installed. it would never raise suspicions because all the bread he had from being and informant he had kept his self-fly. He was young and Rah knew he had a hard life;

however a snake was a snake and they would even turn on their owner so Jab had to go.

Mr. Ass and Mrs. Ass waited patiently for Reese to come into their office, today would be their lucky day Reese would give them everything they needed to convict Raheem Davis and with him in custody he would give them his family. With the information they had on him they knew that he would fold easily the information they already had wasn't enough but when Jab came in they would have their warrant on stand bye. No judge wouldn't except that request after fifteen years they would finally get that big promotion. The whole task force would get a raise.

Anthony and Deedee better known as Mr. and Mrs. Ass walked into the hood deli on Banbridge to get coffee and donuts as usual. The hood hated when they pulled up. They would walk up to the corner dudes and terrorize them for the fun of it. If you were ever arrested by them and no one knew they would surely expose you which caused a lot of kills. They knew it but did they care, of course not it was making their job much easier. "Was sup fellows?" they said trying to harass the dudes in the store but they dudes just walked out. Today wasn't the day nobody had product because LG wasn't around and he wouldn't be around he was laying low. Which was what he always did but he usably left the product but he just needed to stay outta sight. His man was coming but he didn't get there as fast as LG did. He was in some snack and those little dudes had to wait period.

"Oh, so Danny you don't want to be friends today?" they both laughed Danny looked at the duo and just shook his head he had never been arrested nor has he ever spoke to them and what they didn't know he was different and didn't do no bad what-so-ever it was his brother Mark. They knew that but they tried to ruin his reputation by pretending to know him by his first name. The hood knew that because he never did a drill. He would leave but hanging with the crew was just his thing. So, to try that stunt wasn't going to work. Even though LG was his brother and they live in the same house they have never spoke about any of LG business. To be honest he never even considered asking his brother anything because he knew his big brother was in the streets. He knew that if his brother ever became a target for the fuck boys they would try and use him. LG didn't mind him having a life but he told him all you have to do is go to school and I got the rest. That's exactly what he did to.

Everyone in the hood knew for a fact that if Danny ever got caught up in any drama their would-be hell to pay.

To be told though, Danny had friends of his own and they did some wild shit. Only if his brother knew he would beat him senseless, so he was really low with his hood life. "Man, won't yawl just leave me the hell alone, isn't nobody stunting yawl" he said to the officers. "All yawl do is get people killed." The officer laughed "So is that right, Danny boy." Danny just kept it moving but he wasn't about to get far. They wanted to know who got killed and what made him think it was because of them, he just let them know that he knew more than what he perceived to. "So, Danny boy let's have a chat." Mr. ass said walking up on him. Danny took off running. The officers found that to be pretty strange and the chase began. All the dope boys were screaming "Don't run bro, stop bro, why you running?"

Next thing you knew shots were fired. "Oh shit, what the fuck you doing?" the dudes screamed. "Yo somebody call his brother they fin to kill this nigga." 'Block, block, block' this hood was about to be on fire… 'block' "I need back-up, shots fired," the lady office yelled "Officer down do you read me? officer down," she cried her and officer David's has been partners for over ten years and here he was about to die. "Why didn't you have on your vest?" her tears were pouring down. "Officer down, officer down, "she continued to repeat.

Cars were there but the ambulance still had not reached. Officer David's tried to speak. "No don't speak honey save you breath, just breathe help is on the way, I'm going to get that son of a bitch I promise." The hood was in a fucking aww they could not believe what the fuck went down. Did Danny really just man down a fucking cop? This shit just went fucking viral and someone sent LG the video to his phone. "Damn son," one of the corner boys said. "I ain't no boy was capable of no shit like that. They gone kill that boy when they catch his ass. Nobody who kills a cop ever last twenty-four hours in jail boy."

Now the ambulance is on the scene and they did everything they could but it was too late officer David's was D.O.A and just like that the hood would be on ice for nothing they thought what they didn't know was Danny was being bullied and raped by the officer for years because he would never give him any information on his brothers. Officer David's had seen the young boy one day in the lower part of Manhattan he was off duty at a gay spot no one knew he was bi-sexual and so was Danny he knew he couldn't tell his brother he was gay or bi-sexual so he would go to the village where being his self was excepted.

Officer David's looked up in the club and to his surprise he saw Danny with his lover all hugged up and he got low so he wasn't seen and was able to sneak out where he waited for him. As Danny exited Robbie's Gay Lounge in the village he was so drunk he was with his lover they laughed the whole way towards his lover's car where they had sex for over an hour in all kinds of positions. Officer David's was so turned on by the young boy he had to have him and he was intoxicated he lost all control and got out of his car and started walking to them. Before he could get himself over there Danny got out kissed his secret lover and his lover pulled off. Danny just smiled he was full of smiles he hadn't had any action in a while.

"Hey, so look what we have here," officer David's said. Danny was a little confused at first because he couldn't be in the same place as him only gays and lesbians were in that neighborhood. Once he realized his spot was blown by the officer he instantly became sobered up. Was he followed did the officer catch him having sexual acts with another man all kinds of questions started being thought of in his head. "Was sup officer?" he asked trying to be normal, so he thought. Even though being gay was normal it's legal to be free and happy and gay was happy no one had that right to take that away from people.

"So, I am very interested in knowing does your brother Lamont and them know that you're down here sucking and fucking men in their cars and leaving you to take a train he asked with a raised eyebrow." Danny couldn't believe the damn officer caught him in the act. He knew the officer was about to blow him up in the hood. There was no way he was going to let that happen, so he quickly tried a tactic he thought would work.

"First off, I don't think your fellow officers would like to know their friend is a booty boy either," he bravely said. "Ha ha ha," the officer said. "You black punk do you know who the fuck you talking to huh?" he asked throwing Danny on the car in front of them. "So, you like to suck dick huh and get fucked up you rear-end. Well let's see how much you like to be fucked up your rear-end." he pulled down Danny pants and turned him around. "What the fuck man?" "Shut up punk before I take your black ass in for assault on an officer. Remember it's my word against yours and I will always win. I won't get pinched even a little bit over your black ass remember that I protect and serve and I'm about to serve you. Now shut the hell up and give me that ass. If you make a sound, I will blow your fucking brains out." Surprising he didn't make a sound as officer David's shoved his dick up his ass the only thing that made him happy was that it only lasted a couple minutes, Danny couldn't see how a cop could fucking rape him on a damn sidewalk and not one fucking person came walking down the block.

"Now get the fuck out of here you booty boy and you better be here Friday at eight o'clock sharp have some information on Lamont or I am going to rip your asshole opened every day until you no longer can sit and then you won't have no damn choice but to give me what I need and I'll keep your little secret safe forever." Danny knew that was bullshit he walked off feeling so low and disgusted all he wanted to do was go home in shower, he dealt with this abuse being degraded for months at a time. He was so traumatized all he did was go to school every day and come home and stay in his room. No one noticed anything was wrong because staying in his room was something he always did he was such a strong person to be able to hold all that in.

He vowed that one day he would kill officer David's for humiliating him and making him do all kind of sexual acts on him but it would be public. He wasn't a fucking pussy or coward like everybody thought, he was just into his own thing. Yea he had brothers, but his big brother loved him. Yea but he really never showed him the ropes never did brother to brother things anything manly nor did he show him how to protect his self from these mean streets. He wanted to confide in his brother about so much but his brother was always gone and he would never except him for him and because he loved his brother with his whole heart, he kept all the bad things people did to him to his self. He knew that even though his brother was a street runner he loved him and would most definitely kill someone for him.

He didn't want to get his brother locked up or hurt so he held it all in. Danny planned this day down till the t he knew today was officer David's and his partner day and time to roll up in the hood and he would feed him the information to get them on him, he knew he would get officer David's to follow behind him because his partner was there he would have to react to the information. Nobody heard Danny but he told them Jab was dead because of them and he knew it was because of them, that is why they wanted to talk to him. The police had been looking for their informant for weeks but Jab was somewhere floating in the Tampa Bay. They wouldn't find him for a while. He was done taking the abuse from this asshole and him fucking him in his ass then when officer David's was ready to cum he would cum all in Danny's face. Today was going to be the day he paid for it. He would die and he didn't give a fuck any more about life.

His brother wouldn't understand what he was dealing with. He never ever wanted anybody to say to him if it wasn't for me. So, he vowed that anything he did in life only he would pay for it. What he wanted, he would earn it, so he could get it himself, no one could say they brought it. He had so much he wanted to tell LG but he knew he wouldn't understand, better yet they barely saw each other unless it was on the wake up.

They had different dads, he stayed at his dad most of the time but he needed his brother. He didn't have no one to play basketball with, football nor soccer so that just made him isolate and then he changed school and that is when he found his mate which was a guy. The guy listened to him, he understood him. He was so easy to talk to; he could be his self, he had so much hidden pain in him yet not one person to talk too. Danny ran as fast as he could it was shocking that he heard the police sirens so close and not one car in his direction so he slowed down, he tossed the dirty gun in the sewer at least one part he knew more than anyone thought. His lover was hood and he taught him everything he needed to know and things his older brother never taught him. Every part was tossed in certain parts of the hood. Danny jumped on the subways crowded trains of New York and headed to his lover's home where he was already waiting. Danny had called him right before he tossed his burner phone, he didn't need nothing to follow; he would leave town and never returned.

David's partner was so distraught she couldn't even speak she couldn't give no description on the cop killer she couldn't breathe and no one had a clue they were husband and wife for ten years, they kept it a secret because on the force there were no intimate relationships or they would be put in two different police stations. They pretended to have other spouses but they were from call centers they paid the call service for the same person for years, this Friday they were going to the sergeant together and tell them they were married and she was five months pregnant with their first child after ten years, they've tried for years and after three miscarriage's she didn't think she'd ever have his baby. They decided that once things calmed down they would have adopted a child. After finally making it pass miscarriage stage and hiding her pregnancy for five months it was time to spread the news to the whole police force that not only were they married but she was about to have their first child. The officers tried talking to her asking her what happened all she could do was cry, no other words came out. She did manage to point as she rolled over, she began to get pains in her lower stomach. "No please no," that pain she had always felt when she was about to miscarriage, "Aaaaahhhhhh" she was screaming to the top of her lungs "Help me, help me!" the medic immediately ran to her aide, "My baby, please my baby aaaahhhh". "Ma'am how far along are you?" they asked but now she is losing a lot of blood. "We got to get her to a hospital now," as they placed officers Mitchel in the ambulance, they had to cut her pants off she was clearly in labor. Soon as the driver took off the other patron instantly began working, he put and iv in Officer Mitchel and the baby started coming "Aahhh" she screamed louder and louder, the medic tried to calm her. "Just breathe Mrs. Mitchel you can do this just breathe in slowly and out. Drive his thing fast."

The sirens came to life as the sped down the street towards Bronx Lebanon and in that moment the baby was out and screaming and they made it to the hospital right on time. They made it…the medic wrapped the baby boy up and as he finished Mrs. Mitchel was passed out, he checked her body for a pulse there was one. He rushed her and the baby into the hospital, they immediately got attention.

LG wanted to go grab something to eat he was high as a kite but he didn't want to use his phone in case they had a tracker on his phone he knew the police would be looking for Jab by now, he also had known they probably were checking all Rah's contacts to see if there were any other calls he would get from a different number. Unfortunately, that would be hard to do because he never let anyone call him from the same number ever unless it was him bottom line. but to keep them in suspense he only called Rah twice every other day to keep the call record the same but they spoke every day from a different number, so before going to find something to grub on LG decided to turn on the news.

He wouldn't stack no moves period unless he watched what chaos was going on in his town there was always some trap popping off mainly cop killings. He turned to channel seven for a minute and just that fast it was his brothers face flashing on the screen big as day wanted for killing a cop. "What the fuck!" he yelled waking up his banana Barbie. "Nah this shit can't be fucking real. Omg how, why?" he buckled as he saw his brother splashing that officer with rounds. He grabbed his phone and turned it on and ran out the door to his car. "Yo bro please tell me what the fuck is going on. Please my boy split an op bro," he cried loudly "Bro help him please bro there going to kill him bro." Rah hung up there wasn't nothing to say he had already gotten word about what happen it was only a few things to do.

# Chapter 12

"What's wrong how could this happen?" Low cried his son was just kidnapped and his wife died all in one fucking day he was distraught. Reyna was now uncuffed she had spoken to the cops and told them everything she knew. At this moment, she just wanted to die, her life was over everything she loved she had just lost. She felt responsible for Little Low being kidnapped she was beyond crushed that Peaches died in her arms, her and Chica fought, and Candy just died. At this point there wasn't anything her or Low could do besides go home and figure out a plan.

Low was stiff as welfare cheese giving out on a Sunday with a cherry soda. He was so doomed he wanted to just go split his cap off a roof. There wasn't any life in him. His son wasn't even a full day and someone stole his life right from under him; what the world didn't know was he was about to burn this city to the sun, there wouldn't even be ashes once he was done.

"Hey boo come on let's go, we have some things we need to do I'm freaking exhausted and I know you are too, so come on please." Low just looked up at her and he was ready to break her in half, she felt it too but she be damned if it was another episode like earlier with Chica. "Please Low we cannot stay here they will eventually put us out we will be back early in the morning, I promise to see if anything turns up." She reached down and grabbed his hand softly, he didn't resist although he was a little hesitant but reluctantly, he obliged and got up and she and him walked towards the elevator and got on which the ride down was very quiet and long at least it seemed that way.

As they got off the elevator Reyna phone rang, she looked at the number but didn't recognize it. "Who the hell is this?" she said out loud. Low turned to her and asked, "Who is calling?" "I have no clue." so she decided not to pick up. The caller called back once they got out the hospital, "Who the hell, hello," she answered annoyed. "Put that son of a bitch Larry on the phone." "What? who is this and why are you calling my phone for Larry?" Once he heard his name, he turned and snatched her phone. "Who might I have the pleasure of speaking to because I got my own handle no need to touch down shorty," he barked. "Wow so you really are as tuff as you sound you spit box. Didn't your wife just die and your side bitch too and in seconds this monkey boy is about to be next."

Shocking his self, he didn't hesitate to say, "You're a fucking coward and if your beefing with me bring it you international hot pocket pull up." "Look, you thought you would be able to fuck my ass in public you spit box ass nigga. You never know who you're running your shit mouth to, yet you're playing your hands like you got the whole deck in your hands and no one else has a deck. So, until you learn to shut that fucking trap of yours up your little simple mini me will be straight. Now I don't think going home would be wise because the cuff boys are waiting to put the silver bracelets you niggas seem to love for the murder of your chicken tender." he laughed wickedly.

Low said "I swear if you put one hand on my boy when I find you, I will personally cook you for dinner and have your mother and father over for dinner and have them eat you while I watch pussy." "Again, you don't learn you still speak strongly while I'm sitting here with your little moon in my hands, oh and let me make this clear if you even breathe one word of what I'm saying to you to that bitch phone I'm hollering at you on won't even make it in her dreams." Line went dead. Low looked at the phone and handed it back to Reyna without saying a word.

"Low who was that?" and just as Low press the alarm to his car the shit blew the fuck up. Him and Reyna both flew backwards to the ground. This shit just doesn't end does it. Low banged his fist repeatedly on the ground, "I am going to kill someone tonight I swear." All Reyna could do was cry. "What the fuck is going on Low why is this shit happening? Who the fuck was that? Who called my phone?" she cried. "What did you do, please God have mercy on our soles this is too much, please forgive us for our damn sinning Lord; whatever it is that we did, we can fix it pleaseeeee." Low grabbed her off the floor "Let's go, let's go now."

She just cried. How could she just be with her girls having such a good time and then bam all the drama started. "Peaches was killed Low," she said over a whisper "Peaches was killed, she was killed why yo? We ain't never do nothing this tragic for this shit to be going down like this." Low pulled her to the curb to catch a cab he told the cab driver, "Take me off the interstate twenty miles from here to the first hotel you see." "Where are we going Low?" "Look we cannot go to neither one of our crash spots and give me your phone." she did and he tossed it.

She didn't say nothing as she watched him toss her phone. She knew it was a reason and a dang on good one.

She just stared out the window and said a silent prayer because she didn't know what the fuck was next. Low watched behind to make sure there were no cars behind them. He needed to get far away and Costa Rica seemed like a pretty good spot. Only he didn't know he couldn't escape this wave that was coming his way. He looked over at Reyna who was laying there with her head on the cab window. He pulled her to him and laid her on his chest she didn't care all she wanted was her friends back, to get Little Low back before you knew it, she was off to sleep.

Within a minute or so they pulled up to a hotel, a lavish one at that. He woke her up handed her a wad of bank told her to get a room while he used the pay phone. "Hello, can I get a room for two please with two separate beds." "Sure, that will be one hundred and seventy-nine dollars please." "No problem." Low walked in and said, "Make it for three days." Reyna didn't even say a word she just paid the bread. Latrice the hotel clerk, handed her the key to room 322 "And if you guys need anything, you can dial five. My name is Latrice I'll be glad to assist you." They both said, "Thank you." and they headed to their room as they made the entrance to their room they realized they hadn't eaten anything but they were both beyond tired, so they both crashed clothes on and all.

Hours later, Low had waken up to the smells of turkey bacon, eggs and cheese, grits and some biscuits. "Good morning bro," she said smiling. He couldn't believe he slept all night and not realized she had left and went brought breakfast which was very dangerous for everything that was going on. She should have known better but the fact that she was back in one piece and had the joint smelling good he wasn't going to make a big deal out of it right now. He yarned and said, "Was sup, you got it smelling all good in this joint." She laughed, "Are you ready to eat because a bitch is starving." she giggled. For a quick moment he thought about their little fling and he quickly shrugged it off. "Where my plate at, a nigga hungry too word." he laughed. "Next time don't be taking your butt out here unknowing what's out there. It's a lot of fuck shit going on," he said shaking his head as he took a piece of bacon off his plate that she handed him.

"Do you want to talk about it?" she asked looking at him? She knew he may not but soon he wouldn't have a choice, they had so much shit to do. He looked and he said, "Shorty my life just took a major loss," she sat down on the bed next to him. "I know bro but trust me we are going to get little man back, but we have to um you know…" she didn't think those words could even come out her mouth, however, he said them "We have to bury my wife and help burry Peaches."

He turned around and looked at her the tears were pouring out but it was so quiet she didn't make a sound, he knew her heart was broken, shit so was his. He wanted to hug her so bad, yet all he could do was get up and walk towards the window and stare because his mind was going crazy. One minute he was on his way to the show to check out the shit that happen with Peaches, but he never made it because the fucking car got a flat that took a damn hour to fix and then he had gotten a voicemail from her talking about Candy had the baby. So his wife and kid was first and as bad as he felt for not being able to make sure shit was good, he had to go to his wife.

He couldn't take the thought anymore he grabbed his jacket and walked out, at this point he could care less what awaited on the outside for him. His son was missing, his wife was dead and before he did something that would cause major consequences. He needed some much-needed air, his lungs were closing in on him he needed to find some burn. Just that fast he walked into the front desk and down the hall to the vending machines he heard mad noise. Thank God for windows threw out the hallways, there were police everywhere. He prayed they weren't for him but as he looked closer, he saw them squaring up at his door. Unfucking believable! In a flash he saw the officers bring Reyna out while they searched the room. He hated he had to leave her there but she would be fine. There was no way he was going to jail without burying his wife and that was why he sprinted in to action as the police started searching the premises for him but he would be long gone.

# Chapter 13

"Wake up sleepy head," King said to Chica. He let her sleep long enough, shit actually two damn days with no pussy. He really didn't care because that wasn't his motto. He was never thirsty, there were to many hoes out there. He just really wanted to support her; she was really going through a lot and he may not get the pussy now. But just by being her arm she would eventually give it to him and for free. It always worked that way. Females are way too dumb whenever a nigga shows them an inch of support, they let they guards down. If woman stuck to the script men would respect them more and that was that.

He always broke the shell of a hood super star he was the man he would oblige by their needs and that's when he got them money and would make any spit bag submit to the bank. He hated that he had a sister and she was just like that, money ruled her no matter how much he gave her so she wouldn't go that route she still did. Chica looked up, she smiled she was a little calmer but her thoughts of Peaches getting killed and the fight with her and Reyna had was bothering her so that smile quickly turned to a slight frown, yet she had the most popular guy giving her all his attention for almost three days straight.

"Good morning," she managed to say as she began to get out of bed but he quickly ushered her back into bed. He made her two slices of wheat bread with some grits and eggs and a tall glass of orange juice. "Why thank you so much," she was shocked because no one has ever treated her this way. This was way too much for her she couldn't believe he was catering to her this way. She now sees how all these women flocked to him because he surely knew how to take care of a woman especially in the time of need. This gave her another reason to smile. "So, what do you want to do today?" he asked her as he slid the sliding table over her with her breakfast and then plopped her pillows behind her back so she could eat.

Taking a fork of eggs she replied, "I need to call my friend and make things right with her. I was totally out of line I am not sure she would ever forgive me, for this not to mention our home girl had gotten killed right in our faces she died in her arms. How could I be so selfish and mean after all we were all together, I so have to make this right." She moved the table to go retrieve her phone to place a call to Reyna but there was no answer she tried again but had gotten the same results. So she placed a call to Candy but same thing, "What the fuck," yet she tried again then it hit her Low broke her phone, so she probably didn't get a new one. "Damn it. I need to shower and get dress, ugh. But I have nothing."

At that point King was handing her a bag with a few items her had one of his women go purchase for her he knew her style so that was easy and even easier to find out her size all he had to do was look at the sizes she already had on. She was shocked. "Um what is this?" she asked looking in the bag it was two different outfits from Adrienne Vitaminic with the shoes to match each one she was very impressed. "How did you find the time?" she questioned. "Well what do you mean?" he laughed. "You're wondering if I left you, nah. I had someone go pick it up for me. Oh, someone like who, your chick?" she asked quickly catching an attitude. She didn't even realize she was now caught up in his wrath. She stormed in the bathroom like a little girl who missed Christmas and slammed the bathroom door. He just laughed and shook his head, she would now be his he thought life was funny you get out what you give, however right now he had to place a very important call it was unfinished business in the town so he stepped out to make the call.

"Yeah was sup my brother?" he spoke quietly into the phone looking back to make sure no one was around. "Well the plan is in motion I got the kid. He safe and sound baby girl fed him and now he's sleeping. It took a minute, he wouldn't calm down for a minute, however finally little one is sleep. She put up the crib and everything before I had even gotten there with him." "Aight good, so you got to lay low because he will remember your face and you don't need no heat involving a kidnapping because that would lead back to me and them. That leaves me only one thing left to do, kill everyone involved even you. So, hit the way. I'll touch basics with you soon."

Low don't know he fucked the wrong sister over when you hurt mines, I will surely hurt the ones you love. He is such a fucking low life and he didn't even realize his whole life was under surveillance like I was the caged built in, this was the life of do 'em dirty it was his time. He won't last long on the streets, once the police caught up to him for me killing his mistress and leaving his name written in blood all in her bedroom, his fingerprints everywhere and with his gun I recovered from his bedroom closet. He will rot in that jail and I know he has plenty of other bodies on it revenge is so tasty.

He made another call to the doctor at the hospital Low was just dumb. He paid to have his wife die it was all part of the plan, kill her and take his son and raise him right up in the hood he would be Young King. His wife no one knew of who didn't even live in the city came and got him and now they are gone and they would never even see this little man until he was of age, they wouldn't have a clue who he was but he was now Young King, he turned and started walking back towards the room, he would go fuck this bitch like he planned then she would be useful. She was all a part of the plan when it all boils down to it. He knew everything except how he was going to get Rah. He was next on his shit list because Rah's pops was untouchable all together he was on his list for years but shit had gotten quiet until Rah killed his man. He was about to fuck the city up there would be so many bodies dropping the hospital would shut down.

As he walked back in the hotel room, he paused he was witnessing the most purified body he had ever saw. Her body was built perfect, her clam booty was nicely shaped, her smooth skin was enough to make any man want to buy a Hershey with almonds. As she turned around noticing him stare at her in aww the water flew slightly from her hair, she didn't even flinch she just smiled and he walked right up on her from behind and gently pulled her into and gave her body slow kisses she began to squirm. His dick was pressed against her butt she pushed back and his phone began to ring but he never stopped. He picked her up and tossed everything on the dresser to the floor sat her on top all in one motion, he dropped his pants to his ankles and slide his dick inside her she began to moan hard he kissed her and fucked her harder he was about to cum and so was she. He whispered, "One second," bent down while still slow grinding he looked to see who it was the text read 911 he backed up said, "Sorry shorty I have to take this," he pulled up his pants and spent off leaving without no return.

# Chapter 14

Reyna was so confused she didn't have a clue as to why the police swarmed the hotel room and asking her all kinds of questions about a girl Low was dating who was murdered and his was supposed to be the killer. "What the fuck is going on? Get off of me!" she yelled while they proceeded to drag her out her room bombarding her with questions threating to lock her up if she didn't tell them where Low was. She was scared she had no fucking idea Low had a whole other secret life, she knew he was screwing around but she never knew it was serious with anybody else and she would have never suspected he had the guts to kill a female a pregnant one at that.

"Look at me where did Larry go? We know he is here so either you tell us where this baby killing mother fucker is or you will be charged as his accomplice so what's it's going to be, damn it?" the officer barked he was mad. He screamed in her face, "You deserve to be spit on, isn't this your dead friend husband and here you are all loved up with him? You are a disgusting tramp." he went hard on her. She screamed at him, spit flew in his face "Fuck you motherfucker, your momma should have swallowed you in her butt. You don't deserve to be alive you piece of shit monkey." He went to slap her but his fellow officer gabbed him. "Enough damn it, enough she is not our problem if she wants to be a throwback that's her damn problem." he turned around. Search the premises find this cock sucker now." but Low was long gone.

They left her and went on their search of the hotel clerk Latrice went up to her room to check on her, she heard everything the officer said to her and she felt so bad for this girl. "No woman should ever be talked to like a piece of shit," she said to herself as she knocked on the door. "What?" Reyna yelled as she flung the door open Latrice didn't flinch at all. She knew what the girl felt; she knows pain and hurt she never really had a relationship with a man after her first bad experience. Her father warned her never be with any man who disrespected her because if you allow it once it wouldn't stop and her father was killed so she really hated men. She only wanted her dad.

"Hey sweetie," she began to say and Reyna yelled "Please I'll be out in a few, damn just give me a minute please to see if I can make some calls." "Listen I am not here for that I am actually concerned about you. I heard how awful that cop spoke to you and you didn't deserve that." Reyna stood there looking at her like 'bitch fuck you and your fake ass concerns'. "So you didn't come to tell me it's time to check out because my ass is fucking broke? So now let's see how concern your ass really is knowing I can't afford to stay in your fucking fancy ass hotel." and put her hands on her hips.

Latrice laughed, walked in and closed the door. "Look keep your attitude to your damn self, I was actually being fucking nice but fuck it." she said meaning every word. She pulled out an envelope and tossed it on the bed and before she walked out, she turned and said, "Get a new phone and change the number," and walked out letting the door slam. Reyna grabbed the envelope off the bed quickly opening was a stack of hundreds a lot of them almost fifteen hundred dollars with a note attached: Sis I didn't kill the bitch someone is trying to frame me. I'm going to take care of it trust me and get a knew damn phone trust me. I'll contact you and thank the hotel clerk, she just saved my life and stay there for a few more days. Anything you need shorty will get it for you just holler at her you heard. Oh, call Chica and fix it right now you need her and she needs you. I have to find a way to see who is trying to destroy my life and find my boy he is all I got left. I can't go out like this. Shorty is going to get one hundred thousand to you bury my wife right, I want all white doves, a pearly white casket and a bomb ass outfit on her and the same for Peaches. One.

# Chapter 15

Chica was looking crazy King had just fucked her life out and just left without a word she didn't have his number they never even had the chance to do all that.

"What the fuck I don't got my keys, no money, I'm about go crazy." She started throwing everything, she ran and grabbed her phone, she needed to try Candy again she knew she would be upset. Peaches was murdered that she beat the training wheels off Reyna she didn't know if Candy would ever forgive her. Her life was all in shambles and it finally hit her she was alone she sat on the bed and grabbed the pillow and started balling tears.

"My life is supposed to be fun and full of life yet I realize I really never had one," she said out loud to herself as she turned her head to lay it on the pillow there was two stacks of hundreds and fifties with a note: 'Call me shorty in a few weeks.' King had put it there while she was sleeping, he knew he had to go because he had to go attend to his new son Low son, 'Here's my number and twenty thousand." She started counting the money she screamed "Oh my fucking gosh! I'm going to suck the shit out of this nigga dick." Her car keys were also there she ran to the window and there was her baby all shining he had it detailed in all. She beamed, now it was time to go see Candy she knew she would find Reyna there and she was that bitch but she owed her a huge fucking apology and "Biting my tongue is something I am going to do no matter what because I truly was dead wrong," she said as she grabbed everything she needed out the room and cleared.

She got in her car it felt different, it was different "Omg this nigga decked my car out. He changed my seat covers and all what the fuck was he trying to do? Nah he trying to have me living with one of his bitches, nah not me he got me all the way crunk if he thought that was going to be me, sike I think the fuck not, but damn he fine," she said and pulled off blasting the radio.

She was going to get her friends she needed them and they needed her it's nothing like friends, people can say they don't need anybody all they want but truth though, life can't go on with each one pleasing one, true facts she thought. As she pulled up to Candy house she noticed all kinds of police on streets all kinds of unmarked cars what the hell was going on as she got closer, she realized the damn channel one news talking to neighbors. She jumped out the car trying to get to the house as fast as possible the cop stopped her, "What the fuck is going on? This is my damn sister house." "Miss, I'm sorry you cannot go in there." "Man if you don't get your sponged face looking ass out my way," trying to run past the officer and a females officer grabbed her up from behind. "Miss do not make yourself a situation with a murder investigation I will lock your fake ass up real fast and I will be home watching my shows now calm the fuck down." "Get off me what the hell is going on this is my sister house. Is she ok? Why can't I go in there? She needs me." she began to cry.

Something terrible was wrong and she just hoped it wasn't Candy. "Please now, where is she?" At this point officer Blake knew she didn't know anything. "Listen honey calm down and step to the side with me." "Please just tell me what is going on who was murdered." "Look no one was murdered in this house it would have been yellow tape surrounding, however you said the young lady who owns this house is your sisters?" "Yes, now where is she I really need to see her. Well, your sister went in labor and had a baby and unfortunately she passed shortly after and her son was kidnapped and we are her speaking to all the neighbors around because her husband is wanted for murder." Chica buckled she was screaming nonstop this was the saddest thing anyone should have to deal with.

"God why are you doing this, you have taken everything I loved. Why though what did I do to deserve this too, my sister and my dad? Nooooo," she continued to scream this officer began to feel like shit she wished she wasn't the one to bare the bad news but she had to. "Come on sweetie, get up you got the whole world watching," she slowly got up and the news was surely catching this whole sad episode. She got up and walked to her car she didn't want to live anymore she had nothing and no one she wondered where was Reyna?

She just sat in her car for a second she pulled out her phone and decided to call Reyna but a strange number came in. "Hello yeah, who this?" "It's Franky" "Oh hey Franky was sup? I can't talk right now I have had the worse few weeks of my life my best friend was murdered in my face and I come to my friend's house and I find out she went into labor, had her baby and died then her baby was kidnapped, I fought my other friend. I can't talk right now. So, may I please call you back uncle?" "Yeah, but I'm sorry to say this, my great niece was found dead in her apartment somebody killed her one shot to the head." "What who Vanity?" "Yes honey, I know yawl have never met and I just recently found out about her and called you because I wanted the two of you to meet," he cried. "She dead? Oh, my goddess it doesn't end." she hung up. She never wanted to pick up the phone again. That thought quickly ended because an unknown caller id number popped up on her cell, "Hello!" she yelled. "Hey." Reyna said into the phone. "Oh, my goodness Reyna, is that you?" she cried. "Yeah boo, it's me I'm watching the news and you're on it. I'm going to text you the hotel information I'm at. Come now, no need for words I need you as much as you need me." She said "Ok, text me now. I'm on my way." "Ok fine, when you get here just tell the hotel clerk you're here for me, she will send you to me, I love you."

Chica was drained she couldn't understand how so much pain could come into her life like a speeding bullet she wanted to die and as she drove away thinking if Reyna didn't call her, she just may have drove off of a bridge. She turned on her cd and just zoned out all the way on the highway. She didn't know what was coming next all she could do was pray for some kind of peace. How was it that Candy died after having the baby? How was it possible the baby was kidnapped? Who and why would they kidnap the baby and the biggest question was who the hell did Low kill? Is this why they kidnapped the baby? Was the baby okay? Her mind was going crazy. As she drove she decided to turn off the music, she needed peace and some tranquility right now and a stiff hen dog no ice if she was gone get through this and they hadn't even buried Peaches yet. Now they had to bury Candy too this shit was all too much to bare. My uncle called saying his great niece was also murdered; New York was really on fire and she now realizes she doesn't want any more dealings with New

York how the fuck is Candy brothers going to handle this news in jail and her baby brother and her son growing up never even getting the chance to meet his mom.

# Chapter 16

Rah was searching hi and low for Danny where the fuck could he be he thought; he has no friends he searched churches, parks, everywhere possibly and he was nowhere LG kept calling him and the results was the same. "Bro I got you. I am going to find him I promise and I am not going to let anything happen to him. All you need to do is get her baby boy. Before I let anything happen to him I will die first on me bro, you hear me?" Rah had to keep reassuring him he knew how he felt about Danny he may not have kept him by his side but he had him tatted the world knows how much he meant to him, any and everybody knew even if I'm not around, he is to be protected and if something happened to him and someone was around and didn't prevent it, they would surely pay for that. So he couldn't see what he missed that his brother was actually walking around with the heat and killed a damn cop life couldn't had been that hard.

LG gave him everything, he didn't want for shit. Was somebody bulling him? He hated his self for not keeping him safe, this was his fault all he had to do was teach him the script even though it was already written. He just needed to get to the town and fast. He needed his brother safe and out of the states like now he knew road blocks, air flights, and everything was sealed but rest assure he would get his brother safe. Even if he died by doing so nothing would stop him.

Rah phone rang and he almost didn't pick it up because he assumed it was LG and he didn't want to tell him he still hadn't yet found his baby brother but he answered the call anyway. "Yo," he said in a low voice because he knew LG was an hour and forty-five minutes away. "Was sup tough guy?" the caller said. Rah looked at the phone "Yo who this." "Nah nigga I'm about to show you something," and his text message went off the caller said, "Yeah nigga I know that text came through so go ahead and check it. I got a nice surprise for you." Rah checked his messages and it was a video of his father ducked taped beaten badly and chained to a steaming hot oven.

Rah was always taught not to show emotions, it will steal away your soul but he wanted to scream. Rah breathed in and out before he spoke. He knew whoever he was speaking to meant business so he had to choose his fucking words correctly or he would surely make his pop die faster than he was with the wrong choice of words. "Alright you got me, was sup." "Nah nigga ain't no was sup you killed my man and for that your pops is going to pay big time so any last words to your pops because I would have never thought in a million years that I would get my revenge on this punk?"

"See young man somehow you grew up not knowing your family history. Your pops didn't tell you that his bitch ass brother killed my father, did he? Well, guess what he did and then married his daughter and she ended up killing his ass. Yeah so after a few months on giving our family some revenge she gets spotted by your pops and he turns her in and she got the lethal injection. See he was your pops half-brother no one knew of him only your pops. So my ass is going to kill him and then I'm coming for you too. You had my boy being your little flunky it was a good plot he got close to you and you took him in but he couldn't get close to your pops that's all I wanted was your pops but you got on some baby shit and the bitch gripped you for your bank. Had you been a husband to that annoying ass wife of yours I wouldn't be fucking her and letting that bitch drink down all my babies. Lord she drives me insane she just keeps sucking and sucking till there isn't no syrup for those pancakes you love her too. He then turned and blew his pops brains out. That's enough nigga you done," and ended the call.

Rah couldn't believe this, how the fuck did he just witness his pops get killed and it was nothing he could do. Should he have begged the caller but that wouldn't have made a damn difference, boy was going to kill him regardless. He parked on the side stripe he banged his hands on the wheel what the fuck is he going to do how could he go home and explain he just witness their pops murdered. It was too much shit going on at once and none of it was good. His phone rang again he answered quickly, "Yo, Rah please don't hang up. it was Pasha," "Bitch I swear when I catch you and they find you all your body parts are going to be missing." he screamed and hung up. No way in the world she took 200k from me and thinks she can call me I'm going to teach all you mother fuckers why they shouldn't fuck with me, they all must croke over promise you. His phone rang again it was Pasha she really needed to tell him what was really going on but he refused to answer yet she continued to call. "Are you kidding me? Bitch why are you calling me?" he questioned with full of animosity, "Please just listen, this thing was so deep and I'm sorry." "Bitch fuck your sorry." "Just please listen, King has your father and he is going to kill him and then he is going to kill your brother. Dell is a part of this too. He and your brother became cool right under your nose," she cried. "I also have your money stashed away I'm really scared. Yes, it was all a part of the plan until I fell in love with you" she sobbed.

Now she had gotten his full attention "Bitch if I find out you are lying you better never show face again ever you better get a whole new face in all do you hear me bitch?" "Yes." "Now where's my fucking money?" "I have it with me but you have to promise you won't kill me once you get it. I really am in love with you Rahmeek," she said calling him by his government name. He paused, he had always loved the way she said his name. No one has called him by his whole name since he was a kid. "Look where the fuck is you, give me your location. I'm coming in blazing, so if this is a trap your spit bag ass better not be there." "It's not a trap. I swear I am alone I need to get away before King gets back plus, I know the combination to his safe he has over a million dollars in there but please hurry I am texting you as we speak." Rah didn't even respond he just banged it. Pasha prayed Rahmeek would forgive her and not kill her she just needed to get away she knew King was an undercover monster but she had to do what he said or he would kill her and her daughter.

King was a vicious man she knew this for sure no one knew but he was her cousin. She hated him, the only person who knew was Dell so that they could get away with all their dirt and no one has ever caught the three together they pimped females, they used women and made them set guys up. She hated that she had gotten involved with Dell and once she had gotten in there was no way out. It was like a gang the only way out was death. She hoped everything she was about to do would save her life she wouldn't care about nothing else she had enough money in an offshore account she was going to run and as fast as she could.

She was in a bad relationship for too long with Dell and her crazy ass cousin, how could you sleep with your cousin and have a baby with her. King was one sick son of a bitch. She didn't want to sleep with him, for God's sake he was her cousin but they started off as humping as little kids but he took this shit to another level. He raped her when she was fifteen years old, he took my apple and burst it in two and she had gotten pregnant. He threatened if she told a sole he would kill her and her baby and she had to keep it.

Once her daughter was born he made her give her to his wife they allowed me to see her until he had gotten arrested and had to do five years. My parents thought my big cousin was doing a great thing by helping raise her daughter because they couldn't afford to help her. His wife thought she was going to keep her child while he did his bid, hell no after a year she got her weight and courage up, She beat that bitch ass and told her if she ever got in her way again trying to claim her daughter as hers she would kill her and report her ass because she didn't have a green card at the time. She left her and her child alone but he has been home for two years but her baby girl is going on nine years old we need a better life I am so over this shit. I feel sick. Rahmeek texted her said he was minutes away and she better be ready. She was more than ready her daughter was waiting she had no idea how he would act once he saw a child, she prayed he would really spare her life. She texted him and said she was ready and she had all the money out of Kings safe, plus the two hundred thousand she stole from him.

He slowly pulled up in a black four door truck she didn't even give him the chance to park she dragged her daughter and two duffle bags of money and ran as fast as she could, she jumped in his truck while at the same time saying, "Go please hurry! He just called and said he will be here in an hour." "Who kid is this?" he asked because she never mentioned she had any children. "This is my daughter Ria." He looked at her; she was beautiful. "Wow your daughter." Ria looked at him smiling, she said, "Hello, what's your name?" he was stuck he didn't know if he should lie or tell the truth or tell her to shut the fuck up. "Hey little mama my name is Rahmeek." "Oh, hi Rahmeek, I am in the third grade. Mommy says she is about to take me to a nice place to live and away from daddy because daddy is a mean person. I hate him and mommy boy is he scary to. He comes in my room at night, at least it feels like it."

He looked at Pasha he wanted to kill her for what she did, but he couldn't deny he loved her but he had a wife and kids. But knowing her reasons he forgave her and he wanted to instantly protect her and Ria. He checked both bags and as she said they were filled to the brim with stacks. He told her to "Strap little mama up," and he marked off. He knew his pops was dead and now he knew who was behind that voice on the phone, so he would get them.

He just wanted to make a quick call to his wife to make sure they were good then he was jumping on the road to get them to safety. There was no way they could get on a plane or bus safely, not while he was involved. He loves kids, he had kids and to think that this little princess was being molested pisst him off even more.

He was doing over the speed limit, he had to slow down because Ria said, "Mommy, I'm scared why he is driving so fast? Mommy I don't want to die." she cried. He slowed down for a minute and at the light he turned to her, "Hey mamas, I'm sorry. I'm just trying to get you and your mommy to a safe place before your daddy and mommy boyfriend find yawl ok." She shook her head yes and he took off headed straight to the highway. Pasha phone rang, she took her phone out to see who it was. It was King. She knew his call was coming, so she began to shake she wasn't allowed to take Ria out the house without his permission. However, she figured she better answer, so she could stall a little more. So she could be safely on the highway and he would never find them, he had reach but not mafia kind.

Clearing her throat, she answered "Hello." "Where the fuck is you with my fucking daughter? Are you fucking dumb why didn't you leave her here?" he barked. "King she was hungry, so I took her out to eat. I'm sorry she was crying saying her stomach hurts." "Get your ass back here now for I kill your stupid ass. I swear you're just a dummy."

"Yeah ok." she stuttered and he hung up lawd once he checked that safe and noticed everything was gone exactly two point five million dollars, the search was on. But she would be long fucking gone. Like fucking clockwork her phone rang out again. and as sure as Mike and Ike, it was King. She answered she was two minutes away from the airport. Rah pulled over so she could talk he didn't want him to hear the planes, then he would know where to start looking. "Hello," Pasha said. "I'm coming for you bitch. I'm going to kill you slut." she looked at Rah then back at her daughter who was sound asleep. At that moment she pulled out Rah's dick and pushed him back hit the facetime button on her iPhone he excepted and she looked at him and said, Watch this you piece of shit." She began sucking Rah with that sloppy joe head. Rah couldn't believe she was sucking his dick like this. "Shit," he moans "Suck that dick you fucking slut, yeah you know how daddy like it."

She had Rah turn the phone and kept at it. "You fucking bitch!" Rah quickly turned the camera around to his daughter, so he could see she was right there. "Ha-ha," he laughed weakly and hung up. King was furious who was that nigga when he finds out he was surely going to kill them all. Yes, and his daughter he could care less about her. he just gained a princess he didn't want know bitches she would be a slut just like her mama. He needed a male and he had gotten him. "Fuck!" he started banging his head this sperm bank bitch took him for all his bread. He was going to kill her.

He only had twenty-five thousand on him and no more bread. If he didn't get that back, he would need to work fast he had just given his wife twenty grand for the young prince and now he was banked he started making some calls. He would have never thought this ragged fat bitch would do 'em dirty. Truth of it everybody gets done dirty in one way or another and it was his time but she will soon regret that decision. She won't get to spend a damn dime of that money, "Fucking cunt!" he yelled. "Was sup" Dell answered the phone. "Nigga get here now!" King barked but Dell was too busy banging out Nancy, Shocker bitch her pussy was good, really good. He just hung up he would go but right after he came in her mouth, that's why he loved this bitch. He tells that bitch drink up and she didn't even hesitate. Shit he didn't even know she was a freak like that. On his birthday right at twelve o'clock, he brings in his birthday right. He was cumming, he warned her but she said keep going daddy I want all of you and he did just that. He filled her up and she became his boo. He didn't never have no shit like that. And right now, King had to wait. He can pull that tough shit on them niggas over there because he isn't no bitch. Hours later.

# Chapter 17

Low laid up at shorty house with his mind running crazy how did is fucking life just go left that fast. He lost his wife and his little man was missing. The police left several messages telling him to call they had leads on where his son could possibly be. He knew that was bullshit, because they've have never found a missing baby that fast. Shit so many babies had been kidnapped from the hospital and never returned. He knew they were looking to question and charge and convict his ass for Vanity murder. "This shit is wild," he said out loud to his self.

He realized he was indeed followed because how did the cops know to show up there. He was sure he wasn't followed, but he wasn't all the way wrong because if they came to the hotel then he was followed then it hit him, "Shit, did they follow me here?" he needed to get away from this joint. He wasn't trying to get shorty in harm's way, he was actually shocked that she helped him. He was trying to find a way out and she told him hide in the closet in her office and as soon as the traffic started moving, he could make an escape through their secret entrance nobody knew about. Only workers knew about this entrance and you needed a special key to enter and exit.

She jotted down her address and gave him her keys he was thankful there were still some good-hearted woman out there. He was gonna hit that, she deserved some free dick and that was for sure and that is something he didn't do no free dick even his wife didn't get free dick. "Word," he said and he started thinking about the first time they had sex, she was shy, she was scared to take off all her clothes. He kissed Candy softly and he began rubbing her up and down until she started to loosen up. She squirmed from his touch. She hadn't felt that way in a long time she was so scared he could feel it. Her body told him she wanted him and bad but she was so stiff; he kept kissing her until she was completely naked, he pushed her legs apart and he made love to her pussy. She didn't know whether or not she was coming or going. He spread her pussy lips further apart and kept on. He was showing her he wanted her and he went to get up and slide that dick in her but she stopped him. "Do you have a condom?" he paused. "Nah do you?" she said, "No." He got up and began to get dressed. She asked, "Are you mad at me?" He said, "Nah shorty I'm about to spin the block and go get one I'll be straight back." She said, "Please don't leave, you not coming back. Just lay with me please. Tomorrow is another day."

She could tell he was mad, he just sucked cotton candy out her pussy and she gonna say tomorrow is another day, but she meant it. Tomorrow would be there soon and she really just wanted to enjoy him but like she suspected she didn't see him for a while. She would call him but he wouldn't answer or he would pick up and say I am busy, I will call you back and never did. She was crushed what did she do, she used to cry. She missed him so much, he always went to her house after work they would talk for hours but when you a hustler and money calls, he would cut but always came back and put her to sleep. He missed those days, now she had died and he never had the chance to apologize to her, even though she was ruff and her mouth was reckless.

She loved him whole heartedly and his heart was broken he couldn't express his feelings or cry to anyone. They would think he was weak; he had the world thinking he hated Candy. When the truth was, she was his heart he loved her more than anything, but he was too busy following behind the gang. He was the only one out the crew to jump the broom and they clowned him and that is why he went back to his old ways and that made her old ways come out. She began fucking his brother, his real brother talking about do 'em dirty. If he ever found out he would be crushed. He would fuck around and kill his brother and they shared plenty of bitches together but that's his wife, his child's mother; he wouldn't get over that one.

Bringing him out of his zone the house phone rang, so he picked up because she told him nobody has that number besides her father's son but she never met him his name was Dee. They connected through social media and being that he was always busy they never had the chance to get up but he called her here and there. "Hello," Low said, "Is this my new love?" softly into the phone but it wasn't Latrice it was her brother Dee. "Oh my fault homie, she isn't here may I ask who is calling?" Dee said, "Who you bruh?" Low didn't want to cause no more drama so he said, "This is Mike." "Alright where is my sister dog?" "She is at work would you like me to tell her to call you when she gets in?" "Nah I was just wondering why her phone was going to voicemail that is all." Just in that instant his boy walked up, "Yo King, we need to go. The baby we snatched from the hospital, her friend Chica was just on the news. Low face became flushed. This shit can't be real. I know I didn't just here this nigga call him King and say the baby we kidnapped friend Chica was on the news. "Alright boy tell my sis I said call me when she gets home." Low couldn't breathe King this mother fucking snake ass nigga. Alright, wait up what's your name again?" he questioned. "Dee nigga." He hung up.

Was this all a fucking set up but how did he end up at Latrice hotel this is crazy. Before he killed this bitch he needed to know more. Low began to flip upside down her apartment, who was this bitch? King had a sister and somehow, they ended up at her job, fucking insane. How could this be what the hell is going on? He was bugging then reality set in, she couldn't have told him I was here because he or someone would be here trying to get him now. Never would she be so fucking stupid enough to let that conversation between him and his man slip up like this. As he tore up her room he pulled out a box from her closet he popped the lock with no force. There was tons of pictures and letters from her father he began to read one.

**"Hey baby girl I know you don't want to talk about your sister but we need to. Chantal Moore**

doesn't have anyone she really needs you. I could never replace you I didn't plan on having any more kids and neither did I want anymore. You were the only thing that brought joy to my life but I am a man, so when I found out about her, I had no choice but to take a test to see if it was true and baby girl it's true you're a big sister twice and I know your mom had another baby girl. Um I believe her name is Reyna, I'm not so sure that she gave her up for adoption and until you find her, you don't want to accept Chantal but that really hurts me. But I hope by the time I'm released that you find the time to meet Chantal she calls herself Chica. Ha-ha anyway daddy loves you. I'll see you soon! Oh and make sure your big bro Dee takes care of you too. He a knuckle head who doesn't even want to talk to me. I'm glad you found him. Love dad."

Low was fucking in shock this shit is fucking bazaar nah this cannot be fucking possible this bitch Latrice is looking for her sister Reyna that her mom gave up for adoption and her father has a daughter by the name of Chantal Moore, who goes by the nick name Chica. No, I know I am reading this wrong because if I'm not mistaking Chantal Moore is Chica and Reyna is her mom's daughter. Wow! And Dee is King also Latrice father's son. This shit is more than insane. Right now, he couldn't focus on this sister shit he had to get this nigga King and now that he knows Latrice is the main key. He was going to be every girls' dream man. He needed her to get next to him, so he could get his baby boy back and revenge would be his.

"This nigga killed my bitch Vanity and also framed me but oh well, fuck her. This will be the element of surprise and as bad as he wanted to go straight to this nigga and let him know he knows he has his kid, he couldn't because that would ruin everything. But what beef did we have; we never gotten in no smoke, so why he is trying to ruin my fucking life?" he asked his self while rubbing his head. His thoughts broke as his phone rang, it was Latrice saying she was getting off a little late. He was about to tell her Dee called but he would wait.

# Chapter 18

Mrs. Mitchell was hurting, full of joy and sadness. She had her baby four months early but he was alive and going to make it. He was inside the incubator and had so many tubes in him but he was breathing on his own. He was one pound at birth but today they said he gained another pound which was amazing. She finally had gotten their baby and yet her husband was sitting on ice waiting to be buried he was killed by some drug dealing asshole's baby brother. She was about to take that whole family down every last one of them caca doodles. Her son would be in the hospital until he gained the proper weight but she was about to be released and even though she was refusing to leave, her room was full of coworkers as well as outside to ensure her and her son safety.

However, she needed to go do the most dreadful thing, make her husband's funeral arrangements. She didn't have a thought in the world that no one with sense would come for her. No one was ever that bold enough to ever walk up on a cop and take fire. Not in all her years on the force so them being paranoid was senseless she would go home and have two stiff drinks, take a hot bath and cry. Her first love was gone. they took him away. So, before she got in her feelings, she needed to go check on baby boy and go home. Right now she needed to be strong that is what her husband would want and that's what she was going to do. As she walked into the nursery she just looked down at her little blessing and she smiled and next thing you know the baby began smiling and she couldn't believe it he felt her presence.

She didn't want to go but she had no choice her coworker Maine would watch the little one. She trusted him with her life. So, she knew she could trust him with her child. He had a daughter his self that he truly adored she was an adult but she watched him raise her most of her life. "Ok boo mommy has to go home and I'm going to miss you a lot and be good for Uncle Maine, ok." Maine wheeled her out where another one of her coworkers by the name of Supora was waiting. "So, you sure you don't want me to drive you home?" "It's no problem boo." "Um ok, you can drive me but I'm bringing myself back." "Great now let's go I need a stiff one," they both laughed and got on the elevator as two doctors got off. "Ladies," one of the female's doctors said to the duo "Hey." "So how is that precious baby coming alone." Officer Mitchel said, "He is doing fine thanks doctor." "Great now you take care of that little one he is our miracle baby, God bless." and kept going. The elevator door closed and Officer Mitchell's became silent. Supora asked "Are you okay baby." "Oh yeah, sorry girl the doctor is right he is my miracle child." As the elevator door opened it was two men with a new born baby attached to his chest and the other one had a child around the age of two, they had balloons lots of pretty colored ones, she knew her husband would be a good dad.

# Chapter 19

Rah couldn't believe that he was helping her when he wanted to kill her, she had caused a lot of bloodshed. He watched as her plane took off and waved by to her baby girl. She was the reason he didn't kill her and she had better be thankful he wasn't a monster. Now it was time to find these motherfuckers. King was a dead man and so was Dell and anything they loved he would die delivering pain on them; a pain they would feel in their grave. Their own souls would haunt them and they would run from them. They would pray on their way to their grave to have mercy but it would be too late. Rah was paying for his father's doing. His father's brother killed that mans' dad. Now my pops is dead, is this supposed to be my life. I told Pasha to hit me as soon as she landed and was safe. He knew she would be because he wouldn't go looking in Barbados, she and her daughter would love it there that's really where he is from. He has family there, so he made a call and they agreed to keep her and her daughter safe. He knew his wife wouldn't find out because she didn't even like his family. Honestly speaking they were praying he left her. They felt she was too old for him and her attitude was nasty. What they didn't know was he wasn't no better, he was the reason she was that way. She could really careless if they didn't like her, she was a fucking boss.

"Hey, I am looking for room two twenty-four please," Chica said. "Oh hey and your name please?" Latrice asked her. "Shantel", Ok let me phone that room give me a second. Hey, you have a guess by the name of Shantel." "Yea girl you can send her up." Reyna said. They never told anyone their name especially with all the drama going on. They needed to be really careful and move with precision. Something about that girl looks so familiar she couldn't put her finger on it. She knew she didn't have any static with no females. She didn't do drama. "Hey, do I know you from somewhere you look so familiar?" she asked Chica. "Nah I'm not too sure where are you from?" she asked Latrice. "The X and you?" "I am also from the X but I've never seen you before." Latrice laughed "I was born there but I moved out her to P.A. a long time ago maybe a decade ago." "Oh, then nah I've never crossed paths with you this is my first time out in these parts but it's nice meeting you." "Same to you, she is waiting for you enjoy your night."

Something was so fucking familiar about this girl I know I've seen her but from where. She would ask Nia about her soon as she got the chance something was telling her in the pit of her stomach which she began to get sick, literally. She ran to the bathroom but wasn't fast enough. She began throwing up. "Ugh what's happening omg my stomach hurts, my body hurts, she began reaching in her pocket, she needed to get home. So she called her friend to cover her shifted. Chica knocked on Reyna room door twice but no answer. She knocked again this time she tried the door and it opened. Reyna wasn't in sight but there was music playing so he figured she was in the bathroom then she heard noises, she ran to the bathroom thinking Reyna was lip singing and decided to go join her but the sight before her was shocking. Reyna sat there tied to the bathroom toilet. Her ankles was ducked taped as Chica began to go towards her she was hit in the back of the head. It was lights out.

Vengeance was always better when you're the one giving the revenge. The unknown person laughed wickedly this is how you really fucking do 'em dirty. These bitches have been running around doing every and any anybody fucking dirty. Yeah, they wouldn't even ever expect to be done dirty. I'm not even going to kill these bitches. Yet, I am going to fuck with their heads for a while and after I'm done with them, when I tell you they are going to want to kill themselves. They will be eventually begging me to kill them but death wouldn't be coming soon at all. Hell was coming ha-ha. Now let's go check the front desk bitch she should be pasted the fuck out after I put that shit in her drink. Pops always said "Never leave your fucking drink around anyone. People do fucked up shit." "Ha-ha bitch probably somewhere dead," the unknown person said seeing that the front desk was clear. But that thought of her being dead went out the window as he seen she was crawling towards the desk I am about to put a bullet in this bitch head.

Mad flashing light started coming toward the hotel way. "What the fuck. Who the fuck called the damn ambulance?" Because the I was seen by this bitch, I ran towards her and wave my hands in the air to let them know the sick patient was right here, but I would pretend to know speak no fucking English. I am fucking pisst this bleach mixed with pyrromethene was supposed to kill the bitch why and how is this bitch breathing. But soon as they jumped out and rushed to her, they turned for a quick second too long and I was gone there was no way I could get caught up as I turned around, I heard the medic say hurry up we're losing her. I laughed do 'em all dirty fuck it.

# Chapter 20

"Hey little mama how you doing?" Mike asked Candy. She was slightly out of it after she had the baby. Me and my cousin had to get her out of that hospital she needed a new life. King couldn't except his sister going through all that pain. Her moms' had her and didn't want her. She gave her to a friend before he was born. She was older than him by a year. Their mom wasn't ready for no kids and the father was nowhere to be found and my mom up and left Harlem forgetting she ever had any kids. Dreamer raised Candy up like she was her own and somehow, we ended in the same high school. Ms. Dreamer remembered my name and had a picture of us together once my mom had me a few years later she decided it was time she let us meet because she was about to die. It's funny because King was on his way to smash her but once she got there and granny started asking him all kinds of questions like his name and shit. She said her child wasn't going to fuck with some young punk. Once she gave him her name that lady began praising God. It was crazy, she told them both that they were sister and brother. It was sad because she then had to tell Candy that she wasn't her real mom that her mom gave her up for adoption. It took Candy a while to get back in touch with King.

She left the school and she ended up meeting that got damn Larry who had bread. He took care of her but he cheated on her over and over Candy wanted to kill herself. When she said she couldn't take no more she was about to leave him she found out she was pregnant. She was the happiest woman on earth she had been trying to have his baby for years she thought he couldn't make kids and boom she figured if God allowed her to get pregnant with his baby when she was ready to leave him it was meant to give her marriage another chance. She loved Low with no fear, nothing anybody said could change her mind about him so when she vented and they just listened, because if anyone said the wrong thing about Low, she would flip the fuck out.

The last straw was when the bitch came to her on some this is Low kid. Her world was crushed in too so many tiny pieces and still till this day he has no idea she knows that all those missing nights of not coming home he was spending it with his baby girl when the money he was giving her shopping sprees turn to none and the abusive words had gotten worse she knew it was time to save herself from him.

So, we had the doctor stage her death injects her with some shit that stops your heartbeat and had my guy snatch the kid. She was doing what was best for her child she knew he would never stop doing her dirty, so his daughter and his son would meet by accident because she was off to San Juan. He would have never guessed that. Her friends would have to understand that staging her death was her only way out. "Hey boo, yea I'm good little man kept me up all night. I am tired as hell but he sleeping now. So, I am about to take a swim and enjoy it until he wakes up." "Well alright, go ahead I'm going to check on him."

Candy felt so fucked up Peaches had been killed and she had staged her own death and her friends needed her and to be honest she needed them too but right now playing dirty was what it was going to be. He would learn that the next fucking time you hurt someone who loved you would get done dirty. This was going to be his karma. I wouldn't come back until that motherfucker was somewhere rotting in a jail cell. He broke her heart. There wouldn't be any coming back from that, bet that. No one would ever see this coming. Do 'em dirty bitches. She didn't want another nigga, she wanted him but once she was done with his ass and popped back up glowing and shit, he would hate life because he has a bitch to raise and I got his young king. Never think you can out do the teacher. Fuck him and the bitch ass daughter of his he would pay for that. He had her out here looking stupid for another fucking kid while they were fucking married, he just had to be dumb or thought she wasn't going to find out. They say every dog has its day right.

As Pasha looked at her baby girl Ria sleeping on her lap she silently cried while looking at the beautiful clouds. She would finally be free from all the drama she nor her child knows what's it's like to feel peace. She has had problems since before Ria was born it was so overrated. She had the worse life, no one would even imagine. It sure looked good on the outside but having someone raise the child your carried for nine months and someone just takes your kid because they couldn't have kids.

It took a very long time to get her child to love her and realize she was mommy. She had to compete for a spot that was the hardest shit ever. All she wanted to do was be a mom to her child and they took that right from her but God put that plan back in motion and she wouldn't let nothing ever stop her again. but right now, she had some shit she needed to do. So, she got out the pool and grabbed her phone and hit her cousin Chrissy phone. "Yo" Chrissy answered. "So, what's its looking like baby?" she asked

Zamir. "Popcorn popped and full to the top I got that bitch Chica."

"Ha-ha she is a weak turtle neck wearing ass bitch. Girl it's time to do her dirty." "Facts she has no fucking clue what's in store for her ass. She thought she was going to do me dirty and leave Brooklyn, this hoe is about to be done fucking dirty." The both yelled, "Stupid ass bitch." "Now what's up with this bitch she with?" Zamir asked. "Don't fucking harm her put that bitch on a flight. That's Candy, baby girl. I got to let her know I finally got us."

To be continued.......

Thank you for reading. I truly hope you enjoyed. Remember trust no one; everyone will do you dirty!

## About the Author

I was born in raised in the Bronx till I was 13 till I went to

Harlem where I moved with my mom and three other

siblings. I eventually ran to the streets for comfort and

support which lead me to doing a five-year bid leaving two

sons behind. I came home my mom past and was homeless

went into the shelter for a year came out met my husband

and had another son. I have always written and wanted to

be a writer

Made in the USA
Middletown, DE
01 January 2022

57423262R00102